W9-CFZ-947

Milestones
Along the March

TWELVE HISTORIC CIVIL RIGHTS
DOCUMENTS—
FROM WORLD WAR II TO SELMA

EDITED BY LYNNE IANNIELLO

INTRODUCTION BY JOHN P. ROCHE

FREDERICK A. PRAEGER, *Publishers*
New York • Washington • London

FREDERICK A. PRAEGER, PUBLISHERS
111 Fourth Avenue, New York 3, N.Y., U.S.A.
77-79 Charlotte Street, London W.1, England

Published in the United States of America in 1965
by Frederick A. Praeger, Inc., Publishers
Second printing, 1966
All rights reserved
© 1965 by Frederick A. Praeger, Inc.

"Letter from Birmingham Jail" (April 16, 1963) from *Why We Can't
Wait* by Martin Luther King, Jr.
Copyright © 1963 by Martin Luther King, Jr.
Reprinted by permission of Harper & Row, Publishers

Library of Congress Catalog Card Number: 65–24709

Printed in the United States of America

Contents

Introduction

JOHN P. ROCHE

If we are going to understand the development of the concept of equality in the United States, we must first of all establish certain historical propositions, propositions which will provide the framework for the documents contained in this book. At the risk of sounding un-American, I must insist that the most important fact in any analysis is the right theory—though theory alone is not enough. To paraphrase Justice Oliver Wendell Holmes, the status of equality in America cannot be solved by abstractions, or without them.

Thus we must begin with what I have called "American exceptionalism," the fact that the achievement of liberty and equality in this country has been accomplished under unique historical circumstances. In every other free nation, the struggle for human liberation has been one of circumscribing the power of an irresponsible elite—a church, a monarch, an oligarchy, an aristocracy. In other words, freedom for the mass of the population has been attained by destroying the arbitrary jurisdiction of a small, self-anointed ruling class. In contrast, the problem in the United States has always been one of obtaining civil rights *from the majority*.

To put the matter differently, the society which emerged on this side of the Atlantic in the seventeenth and eighteenth centuries outran the authority mechanisms of Tudor-Stuart England. Despite certain rituals, the British provinces in North America were essentially "do-it-yourself" exercises in community building. And by the time the British—after the end of the Second Hundred Years War with France in 1763—began to assert their theoretical rights of sovereignty, these communities were deeply entrenched behind the barricades of local, responsible self-government.

It was John Adams—that brilliant, perverse, and underrated

social theorist—who noted all this and went on to point out
that in terms of elite theory, i.e., who shall rule in America, the
American Revolution was over before the fighting began. And
it proved impossible for the British to cope with the colonists
because the Redcoats were confronted not by a few malcon-
tents, but by a thoroughly integrated society resting on a
foundation of responsible self-government. To win the Revolution a few battlefield victories would not suffice: His Majesty's forces had to crack and destroy a whole social system.

The Americans fought the British for the right to define their
own rights, the right they claimed from habit and prescription
to run their own communities in their own fashion. And the
truth-finding mechanism was majority rule. (This belief pene-
trated all institutions: Pope Pius VI permitted the American
Catholic clergy in 1788 to *elect* their first Bishop, John Car-
roll!) The sovereignty of the community—operating through
the majority—was plenary. Everyone, of course, believed in
"natural" and "unalienable" rights, but the crucial consideration was that the community had the authority to define the
content of these abstractions. The "Peace of the Common-
wealth" was substituted for the "King's Peace," and the result
was that tyranny of the majority so brilliantly limned by Alexis
de Tocqueville fifty years later:

> When an individual or a party is wronged in the United States,
> to whom can he apply for redress? If to public opinion, public
> opinion constitutes the majority; if to the legislature, it repre-
> sents the majority and implicitly obeys it; if to the executive
> power, it is appointed by the majority and serves as a passive
> tool in its hands. The public force consists of the majority under
> arms; the jury is the majority invested with the right of hearing
> judicial cases; and in certain states even the judges are elected
> by the majority. However iniquitous or absurd the measure of
> which you complain, you must submit to it as well as you can.

The rights of man were thus accorded to the American as
defined by his neighbors—a definitional process that could on
occasion be a bit disconcerting. In 1794, for example, at the
time of the discontent over the whiskey tax in Western Penn-

sylvania, Albert Gallatin told some of his inflamed neighbors to stop acting like a "mob." They ominously referred him to a recent resolution which proclaimed "that if any one called the people a mob, he should be tarred and feathered."

With this in mind, let us turn to the concept of equality as it is reflected in Jefferson's majestic statement in the Declaration of Independence: "We hold these truths to be self-evident, that all men are created equal, that they are endowed by their Creator with certain unalienable rights, that among these are life, liberty and the pursuit of happiness."

A masterpiece of political warfare, the Declaration contained no qualifications, no reservations. Yet, if we are to consider it as more than pious propaganda for the American cause, we must immediately supply a number of unarticulated qualifications. Negroes, Catholics, and atheists (to say nothing of the female half of the population) could hardly view this as an act of emancipation. They were not accorded the status of equals in American society, and the men who voted for the Declaration did not rush home to remove their disabilities. A large proportion of the signers were slaveholders who apparently saw nothing contradictory in affirming the equality of man one day and buying a slave the next. (This paradox was not unnoticed; the logical Abigail Adams had written her husband on September 22, 1774: "It allways appeared a most iniquitous Scheme to me—fight ourselfs for what we are daily robbing and plundering from those who have as good a right to freedom as we have.")

If one were to have the temerity to translate this portion of the Declaration into operational political theory, a different proposition would emerge—the proposition which, I submit, is basic to an understanding of the development of equality in America over the past three centuries. It would run roughly as follows—*all those who have been admitted to membership by the political community are equal.* In other words, men achieve equality as a function of membership in the body politic—and this membership is not an inherent right, but a privilege which the majority accords on its own terms.

The myth of the libertarian past dies hard, but if we are going to grasp historical reality, we must once and for all lay to rest the notion that our forefathers built a pluralistic society around the principles of liberty and equality. What misleads many analysts is that restrictions on liberty, and inequalities, were unquestionably the consequence of "democratic procedures"—e.g., an overwhelmingly Protestant society unthinkingly limited the freedom of Catholics and atheists. Papists and atheists were not (in the spirit of the later Smith Act) spokesmen for "opinion," but were subversives, threats to public order. This is not to say that the fathers did not believe in liberty and equality. They believed completely in these great ideals *properly defined.*

Indeed, this proposition was at the heart of eighteenth- and nineteenth-century liberalism. Full membership in the political community, i.e., liberty and equality, was reserved to those who had—in the eyes of the Establishment—earned the right to enjoy it. And in the United States the Establishment was majoritarian. Thus the question to which we are directing ourselves may be put as follows: What have been the historical stages that the Negro has passed through on his journey toward full membership in the American community—i.e., toward acceptance by the majority in the category of "equals"?

Here we must begin with the Union victory in the Civil War and its consequences. The Lincoln-Johnson program of Reconstruction called for freeing the slaves, establishing loyal state governments in the temporarily misled South, and then calling it a day. Those who appreciate Abraham Lincoln's sense of political reality may—admittedly on the basis of spectral evidence—question whether he would have followed this line to its logical conclusion. For one thing, the natural leaders of the Southern white community—though barred from politics for participation in the Rebellion—were hardly going to be eliminated from *influence;* and the marginal political credentials of Southern Unionists made them bad long-run political risks. In short, the power structure of the Southern white community could never be cracked by marginal political figures, particularly those who had fought against the "Boys in Gray."

It rapidly became apparent to the Republican leaders in Congress that the Lincoln-Johnson Reconstruction program was a total failure; nothing was really reconstructed. The Negro, now free, was still at the mercy of the police power and was put into what amounted to serfdom by the Black Codes and labor contract legislation. Worse yet, freeing the slaves *increased* Southern representation in the House of Representatives and the Electoral College. (In 1860, the slave states had seventeen members of Congress "representing" the three-fifths compromise in the Constitution; with the freed Negroes counted per capita for representation purposes, they would pick up another dozen.) Political self-interest, to say nothing of principle—or of the merger of the two that most of us silently manage—required guarantees for the future.

Thus began Congressional Reconstruction which, from the viewpoint of social theory, had as its objective the demolition of the white power structure in the South.

Cracking a social system is not an exercise in rhetoric—it is a campaign which must be mounted with strong administrative instruments and backed by a full political commitment to change. In retrospect, the much maligned Freedmen's Bureau appears to have been remarkably successful. Sent out into hostile country with no conventional weapons for dealing with militant local majorities (only troops, the ultimate weapon in administration), and virtually no infrastructure to maintain day-to-day operations, the Bureau's devoted agents were the unsung heroes of the one effort that could conceivably have broken the social pattern of the South. One who today reads the statute establishing the Bureau must marvel at the institutional genius of its authors: it was an extremely sound attempt at the most difficult accomplishment known to politics—elite building. And it failed not because of its conceptual weakness, but because it never obtained that massive commitment to its goals which made, for example, MacArthur's reconstruction of Japanese society possible.

To summarize, in the brief years of Radical Reconstruction

an effort was made in such measures as the Civil Rights Act of 1866, the Freedmen's Bureau Acts, the Fourteenth and Fifteenth Amendments, to establish a national definition of equality, one which looked to the incorporation of the freed Negro into the political community. But these measures were supported by different men for different reasons and, I am convinced, reflected in the bulk of their supporters a limited conviction that racial equality should be enforced *in the South* for political reasons.

Each nation has its own national obsession; for the United States, racism has been the plague which has undermined our strength and national purpose since the eighteenth century. We cannot tarry here to recount the collapse of the Republican effort to nationalize liberty and equality—the political side of this has been told with sensitivity and perception by C. Vann Woodward. We should, however, examine the process by which the Fourteenth Amendment and its companion Civil Rights Act were converted into battle monuments. This evisceration began in the *Civil Rights Cases* in which the Supreme Court delivered the *coup de grâce* to national efforts to protect the Negro from the "customary" disabilities imposed by "private" action. By giving an extremely narrow interpretation to the Fourteenth Amendment, Justice Joseph P. Bradley (with the former slaveholder Justice John Marshall Harlan alone dissenting) ruled that only formal state action of a discriminatory character fell within the amendment's interdict. Consequently, "private" racial discrimination by railroads, theaters, hotels, and the like was held to be a matter within the sole jurisdiction of the states. Bradley suggested that to rule otherwise would make the Negroes favorites of the national government and would discriminate against white men, who presumably were in need of equal treatment.

The Bradley opinion has to be understood as a period piece. It was grossly unhistorical: the framers of the Fourteenth Amendment were attempting to provide constitutional certainty for the Civil Rights Act of 1866, which penalized racial discrimination by "custom" as well as by "law." In an ironic sense, Bradley's opinion echoed President Andrew Johnson's veto of the Civil Rights Act, which was promptly overridden by two-thirds of both houses of Congress. Fundamentally, Justice Bradley declared the Fourteenth Amendment, as originally conceived, to be unconstitutional.

In terms of the social system, the Negro, even at the zenith of "Radical Reconstruction," never achieved equality. From the viewpoint of the Southern white community, the Civil Rights Acts were a marginal harassment; Union troops were a problem, but the last blue contingent went North in 1877. With the outlawing of "Black Codes," informal measures of social control, which were no less effective because informal, were utilized to the same end. Then, in the late 1880's and early 1890's, began the flood of "Jim Crow" legislation, laws based on the principle enunciated in *Pace* v. *Alabama* that Negroes were different from whites and that this distinction justified differential treatment. Curiously, as Professor C. Vann Woodward has noted (and Tocqueville predicted), "the barriers of racial discrimination mounted in direct ratio with the tide of political democracy among whites. In fact, an increase of Jim Crow laws upon the statute books of a state is almost an accurate index of the decline of the reactionary regimes of the Redeemers and triumph of white democratic movements." The Redeemers had used the Negroes as pawns in their maintenance of political power; now the Negroes were to be punished for their cardinal sin—helplessness.

The classic "Jim Crow" law was an enactment requiring racial segregation in railroad and tram cars. In order to understand the importance of the Supreme Court's decision in *Plessy* v. *Ferguson*, which provided the constitutional foundation for racial discrimination until 1954, let us review the principle involved. When a state required that railroads provide facilities for whites and Negroes on a separate basis, it was establishing a classification on the basis of "race." For this classification to be sustained in the face of the equal protection clause, it had to be demonstrated that separation based on "race" was a reasonable method of attaining a legitimate legislative goal: the mainte-

nance of public health, morals, and welfare. Assuming for purposes of argument that some special "scientific" rationale could
be introduced to justify laws against intermarriage, there
would be no necessary carryover to transportation. One can
require, for example, that men and women use different dress-
ing rooms at the beach without insisting they swim at different
places. In short, the emotionally charged problem of sexual relations present in *Pace* v. *Alabama* was absent in *Plessy* v. *Ferguson.* If the Court sustained the statute, it would be hard to
conceive of any social, economic, or political relationship in
which segregation could not be legally required.

In 1890, Louisiana passed a "Jim Crow" transportation law.
One Homer Adolph Plessy was arrested for attempting to enter the coach reserved for whites and refusing to leave when
ordered to do so. There is an air of unreality about the whole
episode: Plessy was one-eighth Negro and insisted that he was
"white." Like his French contemporary Captain Dreyfus, who
was something of an anti-Semite, Plessy was hardly a fighter
for the rights of man. The Louisiana courts declared him a Negro and he challenged the constitutionality of the statute. Di-
viding seven to one, the Supreme Court upheld the Louisiana
enactment.

Justice Henry B. Brown wrote the opinion of the Court.
Early in his statement, he put the holding in a nutshell: "A
statute which implies merely a legal distinction between the
white and colored races . . . has no tendency to destroy the
legal equality of the two races." After examining precedents
and noting that the state legislatures must be permitted a large
area of reasonable discretion in the police power enactments,
Brown came to the heart of his opinion. The whole difficulty,
he averred, arose from Negro hypersensitivity:

> We consider the underlying fallacy of [Plessy's] argument to
> consist in the assumption that the enforced separation of the
> two races stamps the colored race with a badge of inferiority.
> If this be so, it is not by reason of anything found in the act,
> but solely because the colored race chooses to put that construc-
> tion upon it.

As the clincher to this argument, Brown observed that if the Negroes controlled state legislatures and passed "precisely similar" enactments, white men would not feel they had been assigned an inferior position.

This brings us to Brown's sociology which needs to be set out at some length in his own words:

> The argument [against the segregation statute] also assumes that social prejudices may be overcome by legislation, and that equal rights cannot be secured to the negro except by an enforced commingling of the two races. We cannot accept this proposition. If the two races are to meet on terms of social equality, it must be the result of mutual affinities, a mutual appreciation of each other's merits and a voluntary consent of individuals. . . . *Legislation is powerless to eradicate racial instincts* or to abolish distinctions based upon physical difference. . . . If the civil and political rights of both races be equal one cannot be inferior to the other civilly or politically. If one race be inferior to the other socially, the Constitution of the United States cannot put them on the same plane.

It was precisely in this period that racial theories reached their zenith in the United States; among biologists, sociologists, and social anthropologists as well as journalists and political commentators, the assumptions of Baron Gobineau and Houston Chamberlain—that races were distinct entities and that the white or "Caucasian" race was superior to the others—were taken for granted. The Southern politician, of course, needed no lofty theoretical justification for white supremacy—he knew what he wanted and did not really care how the scientists, journalists, or Supreme Court Justices rationalized racial segregation. But the better elements in the community needed a respectable intellectual base to justify discrimination, and the "social science" of the time supplied the requisite foundation.

Equal protection of the laws was in this fashion glossed by the Supreme Court to eliminate juridical equality of Negroes; essentially, a state fulfilled the requirements of the Fourteenth Amendment if it treated all whites equally, all Negroes equally, and granted "substantial equality" to Negroes vis-à-vis whites.

The Court's holding unloosed a flood of "Jim Crow" lawmaking in all the Southern, and some Northern states, a flood which ended by submerging every aspect of day-to-day life under the protocol of segregation. As Woodward has shown, an ingenious legislator in one state would devise a new law, providing segregation coverage for some area theretofore overlooked, and it would rapidly spread from state to state in a wave of mimicry. It seems to have become a sort of nasty game—and one totally lacking a logical rationale. The same Negro woman who prepared a white family's meals and all but raised its children would be compelled to use the "Colored" drinking fountain, the "Colored" wash rooms, and sit in the back of the trolley to keep the white population uncontaminated.

Indeed, a case can be made that from the viewpoint of the Negro the picture got worse rather than better as the United States moved into the twentieth century. For one thing, perhaps under the impact of the racial dogmas which were so popular, the number of white men who were concerned about the cause of Negro rights went into decline after the Civil War. As the old radicals—Charles Sumner, Wendell Phillips, George W. Julian, William Lloyd Garrison—died, there were few replacements. The *reductio ad absurdum* came in 1903 when the Louisiana Socialist Party came out for "separation of the black and white races into separate communities, each race to have charge of its own affairs."

A second cause of Negro discouragement was the spread of Southern white racial mores into the North and West, a phenomenon which accelerated with World War I and the concomitant exodus of Negroes from Southern farms to Northern factories, or to service jobs in factory towns. The early years of the new century were racked by a series of savage race riots; significantly, they took place in cities on both sides of the Mason-Dixon Line, the two worst being in Atlanta (1906) and Springfield, Illinois (1908). According to John Hope Franklin, more than a hundred Negroes were lynched in the first year of the century, and "before the outbreak of World War I the number . . . has soared to more than 1,100."

The Court decisions offer an insight into the operation of the American constitutional process. Two Supreme Court holdings dealt squarely with the merits of state segregation laws. Yet the Court's rulings in these cases, particularly in the *Plessy* case, were by extrapolation used to validate the whole structure of "Jim Crow." The fundamental question—whether state-enforced segregation violates the equal protection clause—was not (with one area of exception) re-examined by the Supreme Court until the 1940's and 1950's. Thus, while lawyers are technically within their guild prerogative when they assert that a Supreme Court decision is only a determination of the case at bar, the Justices in one "limited" holding (enforced segregation in *transportation* does not violate the equal protection of the laws, *Plessy* v. *Ferguson*) in social and institutional terms gave their imprimatur to the whole structure of white supremacy. In other words, the *Plessy* opinion was a monumental piece of judicial legislation—the Supreme Court effectively amended the Constitution of the United States by rewriting the Fourteenth Amendment in terms of majority opinion.

Gradually, as the twentieth century wore on, the forces opposed to racism and segregation gathered strength. In the 1930's, an increasing number of Americans, appalled by Nazi racial doctrines, began to examine their own social consciences.

Yet, the legal position of the Negro in American life differed little in 1940 from what it had been at the turn of the century. Reconstruction had been closed out by the simple expedient of returning jurisdiction over the Negro to the states, to the "police power," and all efforts to involve the national government in civil rights matters were fruitless. An antilynching bill had rattled around Congress since 1919; on those occasions when it passed the House, the Senate disposed of the issue. (Indeed, Hugo Black's last work in the Senate before being appointed to the Supreme Court in 1937 was the organization of a filibuster which once again doomed the antilynching statute—incredible as it may seem in retrospect, Southern senators acclaimed Black's appointment as a blow *against* liberalism!)

Franklin D. Roosevelt—whose personal views on racism were unimpeachable—seems to have viewed civil rights as an issue which could easily disrupt the Democratic coalition. A supremely sensitive political tactician, he probably assumed that civil rights had little national appeal: he already had the Northern Negro vote on economic grounds, and to raise the libertarian flag could only lose him votes elsewhere.

Thus it was that the United States entered World War II with Jim Crow firmly established in the Constitution, and (one may ruefully assert) in the political and social attitudes of the great bulk of the American people. The major American religious organizations—Protestant and Catholic—carefully skirted the moral issue. The political parties uttered banalities about "equality"; national political figures confined themselves to studied ambiguities which came down to the maxim "Let the people of the states handle it as they wish." A segregated Army, a Navy where Negroes served only as mess boys, and a lily-white Marine Corps went forth to battle the Japanese and the Nazis.

Such is the background of the fantastic revolution in American attitudes that has occurred in the past generation. As the documents in this book indicate, the major event of the past twenty years—beginning with Harry S. Truman's superbly courageous decision to break the "cake of custom"—has been the mobilization of federal authority on behalf of the rights of Negro Americans.

This has not occurred in a vacuum, but has been a consequence of a tragically slow but decisive shift in *white* attitudes. Indeed, crucial to the success of the fight for equality has been the fact that we have had a "White Revolution," not a "Negro Revolution." A "Negro Revolution" would have been doomed in a society 90 per cent white. Great Negro spokesmen such as the Rev. Martin Luther King, Jr., have served as the catalyst, have forced the white community to confront its own conscience. What these documents chronicle is the pattern of response, the institutional responses of American democracy as it moved to close the gap between ideals and realities.

Milestones
Along the March

1. Harnessing Great Power

*Franklin D. Roosevelt Establishes a Fair
Employment Practices Committee—1941*

It was seventy-eight years after the Emancipation Proclamation; forty-five after the Supreme Court upheld "separate but equal" racial segregation; two years after Marion Anderson was refused permission to sing in Constitution Hall—and performed instead at the Lincoln Memorial.

It was January, 1941—eleven months before Pearl Harbor. Huge government contracts had opened the gates of defense industries. There were jobs, training programs to provide skilled workers, the prospect of good wages after long, lean depression years. There was an economic spurt—for white Americans. Negroes saw themselves shut out, barred from many unions, turned away from defense plants, refused "wasteful" training when they would not be placed.

At this point, A. Philip Randolph, president of the Brotherhood of Sleeping Car Porters, took action. He proposed a March On Washington to demand the Negro's right to work.

"A pilgrimage of 10,000 Negroes would wake up and shock official Washington as it has never been shocked before. Why? The answer is clear. Nobody expects 10,000 Negroes to get together and march anywhere for anything at any time . . . they are supposed to be just scared and unorganizable," he wrote in a *Chicago Defender* editorial.

A "Call," issued in May in the name of the Negroes' Committee to March On Washington for Equal Participation in National Defense, told "Fellow Negro Americans" that they possessed "power, great power. Our problem is to hitch it up for action on the broadest, daring and most gigantic scale. . . . Nothing counts but pressure, more pressure, and still more pressure, through the tactic and strategy of broad, organized, aggressive mass action behind the vital and important issues of the Negro."

As the date set for the March—July 1—drew near, it appeared that more than 50,000 American Negroes, neither "scared" nor "unorganizable," were ready to answer the "Call." Randolph and the March on Washington Committee were invited to Washington.

The result became clear on June 25, when President Roosevelt issued Executive Order 8802: "There shall be no discrimination in the employment of workers in defense industries and in Government because of race, creed, color, or national origin. . . . It is the duty of employers and labor organizations . . . to provide for the full and equitable participation of all workers." Clauses forbidding racial discrimination were inserted in all government defense contracts; the President's Fair Employment Practices Committee was established. And the March On Washington was called off—one week before it was to take place.

The wartime FEPC was hailed as the second Emancipation Proclamation. With no enforcement powers, it relied largely on moral suasion and the pressure of public opinion. It suffered from lack of funds and a lack of cooperation from other government agencies. By 1945, it was almost inactive. But before it died in 1946, it had handled over 10,000 complaints and, against tremendous odds, had managed to achieve an imposing score of successes. There were Northern plants which dropped the color bar completely, Western and Southern ones which modified discriminatory hiring practices rather than face FEPC charges.

The threat of the march was effective. It taught Negro leadership a valuable lesson—what "power, great power . . . pressure, more pressure, and still more pressure" could do. It was a lesson not to be forgotten.

EXECUTIVE ORDER 8802

REAFFIRMING POLICY OF FULL PARTICIPA-
TION IN THE DEFENSE PROGRAM BY ALL
PERSONS, REGARDLESS OF RACE, CREED,
COLOR, OR NATIONAL ORIGIN, AND DI-
RECTING CERTAIN ACTION IN FURTHER-
ANCE OF SAID POLICY

Whereas it is the policy of the United States to encourage full participation in the national defense program by all citizens of the United States, regardless of race, creed, color, or national origin, in the firm belief that the democratic way of life within the Nation can be defended successfully only with the help and support of all groups within its borders; and

Whereas there is evidence that available and needed workers have been barred from employment in industries engaged in defense production solely because of considerations of race, creed, color, or national origin, to the detriment of workers' morale and of national unity:

Now, therefore, by virtue of the authority vested in me by the Constitution and the statutes, and as a prerequisite to the successful conduct of our national defense production effort, I do hereby reaffirm the policy of the United States that there shall be no discrimination in the employment of workers in defense industries or government because of race, creed, color, or national origin, and I do hereby declare that it is the duty of employers and of labor organizations, in furtherance of said policy and of this order, to provide for the full and equitable participation of all workers in defense industries, without discrimination because of race, creed, color, or national origin;

And it is hereby ordered as follows:

1. All departments and agencies of the Government of the United States concerned with vocational and training programs for defense production shall take special measures appropriate

to assure that such programs are administered without discrimination because of race, creed, color, or national origin;

2. All contracting agencies of the Government of the United States shall include in all defense contracts hereafter negotiated by them a provision obligating the contractor not to discriminate against any worker because of race, creed, color, or national origin;

3. There is established in the Office of Production Management a Committee on Fair Employment Practices, which shall consist of a chairman and four other members to be appointed by the President. The Chairman and members of the Committee shall serve as such without compensation but shall be entitled to actual and necessary transportation, subsistence and other expenses incidental to performance of their duties. The Committee shall receive and investigate complaints of discrimination in violation of the provisions of this order and shall take appropriate steps to redress grievances which it finds to be valid. The Committee shall also recommend to the several departments and agencies of the Government of the United States and to the President all measures which may be deemed by it necessary or proper to effectuate the provisions of this order.

FRANKLIN D. ROOSEVELT

THE WHITE HOUSE
June 25, 1941

2. To Secure These Rights

Harry S. Truman Creates the President's Committee on Civil Rights—1946

World War II was over, the enemies abroad defeated. The death of Franklin D. Roosevelt had catapulted Harry S. Truman into the Presidency—and civil rights advocates were apprehensive. Their catalyst was gone. A political unknown sat at his desk.

The crusade for equality continued, primarily in the hands of Negro and white civil rights organizations aiming as best they could at specific targets—now discrimination in housing, now education, now employment. They talked of closing the gap between democracy's promise and its reality, but even the most hopeful could see no immediate reason for optimism.

Then, twenty months after he had taken office, President Truman provided a reason—Executive Order 9808, establishing the President's Committee on Civil Rights. He asked for a study on the conditions of American democracy, a written report, and the Committee's recommendations for "more adequate and effective means and procedures for the protection of the civil rights of the people of the United States."

The report, *To Secure These Rights,* was submitted in 1947. It was a candid and definitive critique of the nation's deficiencies, majestic in its honesty, blunt in its recommendations. It charged that the right to safety and security of the person against bondage, lawless violence, arbitrary arrest and punishment was being denied to great numbers of Negroes; it found that serious violations of civil rights prevailed in all sections of the country; that "the protection of civil rights is a national problem which affects everyone."

The Committee asked the Federal Government to take the lead in destroying racial discrimination. It stressed the need for federal legislation to strengthen inadequate civil rights statutes dating back to 1866, and offered twenty-seven recommendations for such legislation. It urged a federal antilynching act; repeal of poll taxes; legislation punishing any interference with the right to vote; modification of naturalization laws in order to grant citizenship without regard to race, color, or national origin; a federal Fair Employment Practices Act, and similar legislation by the states; state laws establishing fair education practices; the outlawing of restrictive covenants in real estate; the abolition of Jim Crow in interstate commerce.

Reaction was varied. The Committee's recommendations were called "thrilling," "dynamite," and "political suicide." On February 2, 1948, President Truman asked Congress to enact the civil rights program embodied in the report. It was the Eightieth Congress, later to be criticized by Mr. Truman during the 1948 election campaign for its "do-nothing" record on civil rights. But if Congress did nothing to implement the Committee's recommendations, cities and states did. *To Secure These Rights* was the inspiration for state laws and municipal ordinances barring various forms of discrimination. New York, the pioneer in establishing a state FEPC, now continued to lead the way with a 1948 statute forbidding discrimination on the basis of race, color, religion, creed, or national origin in institutions of higher education. Connecticut initiated legislation against discrimination in public or publicly supported housing.

The road was clear for progress. Civil rights was now a national issue, injected into the American conscience, dumped into the laps of government leaders—federal, state, and local. It was going to be a long march but, at least, another milestone had been reached.

EXECUTIVE ORDER 9808
ESTABLISHING THE PRESIDENT'S COMMITTEE ON CIVIL RIGHTS

Whereas the preservation of civil rights guaranteed by the Constitution is essential to domestic tranquility, national security, the general welfare, and the continued existence of our free institutions; and

Whereas the action of individuals who take the law into their own hands and inflict summary punishment and wreak personal vengeance is subversive of our democratic system of law enforcement and public criminal justice, and gravely threatens our form of government; and

Whereas it is essential that all possible steps be taken to safeguard our civil rights:

Now, therefore, by virtue of the authority vested in me as President of the United States by the Constitution and the statutes of the United States, it is hereby ordered as follows:

1. There is hereby created a committee to be known as the President's Committee on Civil Rights, which shall be composed of the following-named members, who shall serve without compensation:

Mr. C. E. Wilson, chairman; Mrs. Sadie T. Alexander, Mr. James B. Carey, Mr. John S. Dickey, Mr. Morris L. Ernst, Rabbi Roland B. Gittelsohn, Dr. Frank P. Graham, The Most Reverend Francis J. Haas, Mr. Charles Luckman, Mr. Francis P. Matthews, Mr. Franklin D. Roosevelt, Jr., The Right Reverend Henry Knox Sherrill, Mr. Boris Shishkin, Mrs. M. E. Tilly, Mr. Channing H. Tobias.

2. The Committee is authorized on behalf of the President to inquire into and to determine whether and in what respect current law-enforcement measures and the authority and means possessed by Federal, State, and local governments may be strengthened and improved to safeguard the civil rights of the people.

3. All executive departments and agencies of the Federal

Government are authorized and directed to cooperate with the Committee in its work, and to furnish the Committee such information or the services of such persons as the Committee may require in the performance of its duties.

4. When requested by the Committee to do so, persons employed in any of the executive departments and agencies of the Federal Government shall testify before the Committee and shall make available for the use of the Committee such documents and other information as the Committee may require.

5. The Committee shall make a report of its studies to the President in writing, and shall in particular make recommendations with respect to the adoption or establishment, by legislation or otherwise, of more adequate and effective means and procedures for the protection of the civil rights of the people of the United States.

6. Upon rendition of its report to the President, the Committee shall cease to exist, unless otherwise determined by further Executive Order.

HARRY S. TRUMAN

THE WHITE HOUSE
December 5, 1946

EXTRACTS FROM THE REPORT OF THE PRESIDENT'S COMMITTEE ON CIVIL RIGHTS

I. TO STRENGTHEN THE MACHINERY FOR THE PROTECTION OF CIVIL RIGHTS, THE PRESIDENT'S COMMITTEE RECOMMENDS:

1. The reorganization of the Civil Rights Section of the Department of Justice to provide for:
   The establishment of regional offices;
   A substantial increase in its appropriation and staff to enable it to engage in more extensive research and to act more effectively to prevent civil rights violations;
   An increase in investigative action in the absence of complaints;
   The greater use of civil sanctions;
   Its elevation to the status of a full division in the Department of Justice.
2. The establishment within the FBI of a special unit of investigators trained in civil rights work.
3. The establishment by the state governments of law enforcement agencies comparable to the federal Civil Rights Section.
4. The establishment of a permanent Commission on Civil Rights in the Executive Office of the President, preferably by Act of Congress;
   And the simultaneous creation of a Joint Standing Committee on Civil Rights in Congress.
5. The establishment by the states of permanent commissions on civil rights to parallel the work of the federal Commission at the state level.
6. The increased professionalization of state and local police forces.

II. To STRENGTHEN THE RIGHT TO SAFETY AND SECURITY
OF THE PERSON, THE PRESIDENT'S COMMITTEE
RECOMMENDS:

1. The enactment by Congress of new legislation to supplement Section 51 of Title 18 of the United States Code which would impose the same liability on one person as is now imposed by that statute on two or more conspirators.
2. The amendment of Section 51 to remove the penalty provision which disqualifies persons convicted under the Act from holding public office.
3. The amendment of Section 52 to increase the maximum penalties that may be imposed under it from a $1,000 fine and a one-year prison term to a $5,000 fine and a ten-year prison term, thus bringing its penalty provisions into line with those in Section 51.
4. The enactment by Congress of a new statute, to supplement Section 52, specifically directed against police brutality and related crimes.
5. The enactment by Congress of an antilynching act.
6. The enactment by Congress of a new criminal statute on involuntary servitude, supplementing Sections 443 and 444 of Title 18 of the United States Code.
7. A review of our wartime evacuation and detention experience looking toward the development of a policy which will prevent the abridgment of civil rights of any person or groups because of race or ancestry.
8. Enactment by Congress of legislation establishing a procedure by which claims of evacuees for specific property and business losses resulting from the wartime evacuation can be promptly considered and settled.

III. To STRENGTHEN THE RIGHT TO CITIZENSHIP AND ITS PRIVILEGES, THE PRESIDENT'S COMMITTEE RECOMMENDS:

1. Action by the states or Congress to end poll taxes as a voting prerequisite.
2. The enactment by Congress of a statute protecting the right of qualified persons to participate in federal primaries and elections against interference by public officers and private persons.
3. The enactment by Congress of a statute protecting the right to qualify for, or participate in, federal or state primaries or elections against discriminatory action by state officers based on race or color, or depending on any other unreasonable classification of persons for voting purposes.
4. The enactment by Congress of legislation establishing local self-government for the District of Columbia; and the amendment of the Constitution to extend suffrage in presidential elections, and representation in Congress to District residents.
5. The granting of suffrage by the States of New Mexico and Arizona to their Indian citizens.
6. The modification of the federal naturalization laws to permit the granting of citizenship without regard to the race, color, or national origin of applicants.
7. The repeal by the states of laws discriminating against aliens who are ineligible for citizenship because of race, color, or national origin.
8. The enactment by Congress of legislation granting citizenship to the people of Guam and American Samoa.
9. The enactment by Congress of legislation, followed by appropriate administrative action, to end immediately all discrimination and segregation based on race, color, creed, or national origin, in the organization and activities of all branches of the Armed Services.
10. The enactment by Congress of legislation providing that no

member of the armed forces shall be subject to discrimination of any kind by any public authority or place of public accommodation, recreation, transportation, or other service or business.

IV. To strengthen the right to freedom of conscience and expression, the President's Committee recommends:

1. The enactment by Congress and the state legislatures of legislation requiring all groups, which attempt to influence public opinion, to disclose the pertinent facts about themselves through systematic registration procedures.
2. Action by Congress and the executive branch clarifying the loyalty obligations of federal employees, and establishing standards and procedures by which the civil rights of public workers may be scrupulously maintained.

V. To strengthen the right to equality of opportunity, the President's Committee recommends:

1. In general:
   The elimination of segregation, based on race, color, creed, or national origin, from American life.

   The conditioning by Congress of all federal grants-in-aid and other forms of federal assistance to public or private agencies for any purpose on the absence of discrimination and segregation based on race, color, creed, or national origin.
2. For employment:
   The enactment of a federal Fair Employment Practice Act prohibiting all forms of discrimination in private employment, based on race, color, creed, or national origin;

   The enactment by the states of similar laws;

The issuance by the President of a mandate against discrimination in government employment and the creation of adequate machinery to enforce this mandate.

3. For education:

Enactment by the state legislatures of fair educational practice laws for public and private educational institutions, prohibiting discrimination in the admission and treatment of students based on race, color, creed, or national origin.

4. For housing:

The enactment by the states of laws outlawing restrictive covenants;

Renewed court attack, with intervention by the Department of Justice, upon restrictive covenants.

5. For health services:

The enactment by the states of fair health practice statutes forbidding discrimination and segregation based on race, creed, color, or national origin, in the operation of public or private health facilities.

6. For public services:

The enactment by Congress of a law stating that discrimination and segregation, based on race, color, creed, or national origin, in the rendering of all public services by the national government is contrary to public policy;

The enactment by the states of similar laws;

The establishment by act of Congress or executive order of a unit in the federal Bureau of the Budget to review the execution of all government programs, and the expenditures of all government funds, for compliance with the policy of nondiscrimination;

The enactment by Congress of a law prohibiting discrimination or segregation, based on race, color, creed, or national origin, in interstate transportation and all the facilities thereof, to apply against both public officers and the employees of private transportation companies;

The enactment by the states of laws guaranteeing equal access to places of public accommodation, broadly defined, for persons of all races, colors, creeds, and national origins.

7. For the District of Columbia:

The enactment by Congress of legislation to accomplish the following purposes in the District;

Prohibition of discrimination and segregation, based on race, color, creed, or national origin, in all public or publicly supported hospitals, parks, recreational facilities, housing projects, welfare agencies, penal institutions, and concessions on public property;

The prohibition of segregation in the public school system of the District of Columbia;

The establishment of a fair educational practice program directed against discrimination, based on race, color, creed, or national origin, in the admission of students to private educational institutions;

The establishment of a fair health practice program forbidding discrimination and segregation by public or private agencies, based on race, color, creed, or national origin, with respect to the training of doctors and nurses, the admission of patients to hospitals, clinics, and similar institutions, and the right of doctors and nurses to practice in hospitals;

The outlawing of restrictive covenants;

Guaranteeing equal access to places of public accommodation, broadly defined, to persons of all races, colors, creeds, and national origins.

8. The enactment by Congress of legislation ending the system of segregation in the Panama Canal Zone.

VI. To RALLY THE AMERICAN PEOPLE TO THE SUPPORT OF
A CONTINUING PROGRAM TO STRENGTHEN CIVIL RIGHTS,
THE PRESIDENT'S COMMITTEE RECOMMENDS:

A long term campaign of public education to inform the people of the civil rights to which they are entitled and which they owe to one another.

The most important educational task in this field is to give the public living examples of civil rights in operation. This is the purpose of our recommendations which have gone before. But there still remains the job of driving home to the public the nature of our heritage, the justification of civil rights and the need to end prejudice. This is a task which will require the co-operation of the federal, state, and local governments and of private agencies. We believe that the permanent Commission on Civil Rights should take the leadership in serving as the co-ordinating body. The activities of the permanent Commission in this field should be expressly authorized by Congress and funds specifically appropriated for them.

Aside from the education of the general public, the government has immediate responsibility for an internal civil rights campaign for its more than two million employees. This might well be an indispensable first step in a large campaign. Moreover, in the armed forces, an opportunity exists to educate men while in service. The armed forces should expand efforts, already under way, to develop genuinely democratic attitudes in officers and enlisted men.

3. Opening Up Neighborhoods

The Supreme Court Rules That Restrictive Covenants Cannot Be Enforced—1948

The cities of postwar America were overflowing. A postwar building boom was about to relieve severe housing shortages. There was the beginning of a mass exodus to the suburbs—50' x 100' plots of land, grass, trees, ranch, and Cape Cod homes.

But for Negroes and other minority group members crowded into tenements, there was little hope for change, little opportunity to escape. The hundreds of Harlems across the country were tightly drawn black belts, locked closed by racial prejudice, reinforced by restrictive covenants backed by law.

Restrictive covenants were private contracts, agreements that property would not be sold, leased, or rented to Negroes, Jews, "Orientals," or whatever group was deemed "undesirable" by local prejudice.

Historically, the covenants were both legal and useful. The right of private ownership carried a concomitant privilege which allowed property owners to band together and, by mutual agreement, restrict their neighborhoods from uses detrimental to health or comfort. But limitations on the *use* of property became limitations on the *users*—whole groups of people seeking homes were kept out, branded "undesirables."

Lower courts had generally upheld the covenants as conforming with a "public policy" that affirmed the inviolability of private contracts. Only two cases involving enforcement of such agreements had been brought before the Supreme Court. The first, in 1926, involved two white property owners in Washington, D.C. One had broken a restrictive covenant against selling to Negroes; the other sued in the lower courts, and won. The NAACP carried the case to the Supreme Court, where it was dismissed for lack of jurisdiction.

The second case, in 1940, was an appeal against the judgment of an Illinois state court which had upheld the right of white property owners to honor a restrictive covenant against Negroes. Here the Supreme Court reversed the decision, but on the ground that the Negro petitioners had been denied due process of law. It made no comment on the constitutionality of restrictive covenants as such.

The President's Committee on Civil Rights called for the outlawing of restrictive covenants. Their effectiveness, the Committee said, "depends in the last analysis on court orders enforcing the private agreement. The power of the state is thus utilized to bolster discriminatory practices. We would hold this belief under any circumstances; under present conditions, when severe housing shortages are already causing hardships for many people of the country, we are especially emphatic in recommending measures to alleviate the situation." It urged "renewed court attack, with intervention by the Department of Justice, upon restrictive covenants."

On May 3, 1948, in a case known as *Shelley* v. *Kraemer*, the Supreme Court ruled restrictive covenants to be unenforceable. Such covenants, when enforced, the Court said, deny to excluded groups the equal protection of the laws guaranteed by the Fourteenth Amendment. The Department of Justice had intervened in the case—appearing before the Court to argue the unconstitutionality of the covenants. (Five years later—in 1953—the Court was to expand its ruling, holding that the covenants could not be enforced even indirectly by damage suits brought against individuals who had violated them.)

Restrictive covenants were no longer a weapon to keep neighborhoods segregated. There were other weapons, to be sure, but the legal foundation of residential segregation had been cracked.

SHELLEY et ux. v. KRAEMER et ux.

Mr. Chief Justice Vinson delivered the opinion of the Court.

These cases present for our consideration questions relating to the validity of court enforcement of private agreements, generally described as restrictive covenants, which have as their purpose the exclusion of persons of designated race or color from the ownership or occupancy of real property. Basic constitutional issues of obvious importance have been raised.

The first of these cases comes to this Court on certiorari to the Supreme Court of Missouri. On February 16, 1911, thirty out of a total of thirty-nine owners of property fronting both sides of Labadie Avenue between Taylor Avenue and Cora Avenue in the city of St. Louis, signed an agreement, which was subsequently recorded, providing in part:

". . . the said property is hereby restricted to the use and occupancy for the term of Fifty (50) years from this date, so that it shall be a condition all the time and whether recited and referred to as [sic] not in subsequent conveyances and shall attach to the land, as a condition precedent to the sale of the same, that hereafter no part of said property or any portion thereof shall be, for said term of Fifty-years, occupied by any person not of the Caucasian race, it being intended hereby to restrict the use of said property for said period of time against the occupancy as owners or tenants of any portion of said property for resident or other purpose by people of the Negro or Mongolian Race."

The entire district described in the agreement included fifty-seven parcels of land. The thirty owners who signed the agreement held title to forty-seven parcels, including the particular parcel involved in this case. At the time the agreement was signed, five of the parcels in the district were owned by Negroes. One of those had been occupied by Negro families since 1882, nearly thirty years before the restrictive agreement was executed. The trial court found that owners of seven out of nine homes on the south side of Labadie Avenue, within the restricted district and "in the immediate vicinity" of the premises in question, had failed to sign the restrictive agreement in 1911. At the time this action was brought, four of the premises were occupied by Negroes, and had been so occupied for periods ranging from twenty-three to sixty-three years. A fifth parcel had been occupied by Negroes until a year before this suit was instituted.

On August 11, 1945, pursuant to a contract of sale, petitioners Shelley, who are Negroes, for valuable consideration received from one Fitzgerald a warranty deed to the parcel in question. The trial court found that petitioners had no actual knowledge of the restrictive agreement at the time of the purchase.

On October 9, 1945, respondents, as owners of other property subject to the terms of the restrictive covenant, brought suit in the Circuit Court of the city of St. Louis praying that petitioners Shelley be restrained from taking possession of the property and that judgment be entered divesting title out of petitioners Shelley and revesting title in the immediate grantor or in such other person as the court should direct. The trial court denied the requested relief on the ground that the restrictive agreement, upon which respondents based their action, had never become final and complete because it was the intention of the parties to that agreement that it was not to become effective until signed by all property owners in the district, and signatures of all the owners had never been obtained.

The Supreme Court of Missouri sitting *en banc* reversed and directed the trial court to grant the relief for which respondents had prayed. That court held the agreement effective and concluded that enforcement of its provisions violated no rights guaranteed to petitioners by the Federal Constitution. At the time the court rendered its decision, petitioners were occupying the property in question.

The second of the cases under consideration comes to this

Court from the Supreme Court of Michigan. The circumstances presented do not differ materially from the Missouri case. In June, 1934, one Ferguson and his wife, who then owned the property located in the city of Detroit which is involved in this case, executed a contract providing in part:

"This property shall not be used or occupied by any person or persons except those of the Caucasian race.

"It is further agreed that this restriction shall not be effective unless at least eighty per cent of the property fronting on both sides of the street in the block where our land is located is subjected to this or a similar restriction."

The agreement provided that the restrictions were to remain in effect until January 1, 1960. The contract was subsequently recorded; and similar agreements were executed with respect to eighty per cent of the lots in the block in which the property in question is situated.

By deed dated November 30, 1944, petitioners, who were found by the trial court to be Negroes, acquired title to the property and thereupon entered into its occupancy. On January 30, 1945, respondents, as owners of property subject to the terms of the restrictive agreement, brought suit against petitioners in the Circuit Court of Wayne County. After a hearing, the court entered a decree directing petitioners to move from the property within ninety days. Petitioners were further enjoined and restrained from using or occupying the premises in the future. On appeal, the Supreme Court of Michigan affirmed, deciding adversely to petitioners' contentions that they had been denied rights protected by the Fourteenth Amendment.

Petitioners have placed primary reliance on their contentions, first raised in the state courts, that judicial enforcement of the restrictive agreements in these cases has violated rights guaranteed to petitioners by the Fourteenth Amendment of the Federal Constitution and Acts of Congress passed pursuant to that Amendment. Specifically, petitioners urge that they have been denied the equal protection of the laws, deprived of property without due process of law, and have been denied privileges and immunities of citizens of the United States. We pass to a consideration of those issues. . . .

III

. . . We are called upon to consider whether enforcement by state courts of the restrictive agreements in these cases may be deemed to be the acts of those States; and, if so, whether that action has denied these petitioners the equal protection of the laws which the Amendment was intended to insure.

We have no doubt that there has been state action in these cases in the full and complete sense of the phrase. The undisputed facts disclose that petitioners were willing purchasers of properties upon which they desired to establish homes. The owners of the properties were willing sellers; and contracts of sale were accordingly consummated. It is clear that but for the active intervention of the state courts, supported by the full panoply of state power, petitioners would have been free to occupy the properties in question without restraint.

These are not cases, as has been suggested, in which the States have merely abstained from action, leaving private individuals free to impose such discriminations as they see fit. Rather, these are cases in which the States have made available to such individuals the full coercive power of government to deny to petitioners, on the grounds of race or color, the enjoyment of property rights in premises which petitioners are willing and financially able to acquire and which the grantors are willing to sell. The difference between judicial enforcement and nonenforcement of the restrictive covenants is the difference to petitioners between being denied rights of property available to other members of the community and being accorded full enjoyment of those rights on an equal footing.

[10-12] The enforcement of the restrictive agreements by the state courts in these cases was directed pursuant to the common-law policy of the States as formulated by those courts in earlier decisions. In the Missouri case, enforcement of the

covenant was directed in the first instance by the highest court of the State after the trial court had determined the agreement to be invalid for want of the requisite number of signatures. In the Michigan case, the order of enforcement by the trial court was affirmed by the highest state court. The judicial action in each case bears the clear and unmistakable imprimatur of the State. We have noted that previous decisions of this Court have established the proposition that judicial action is not immunized from the operation of the Fourteenth Amendment simply because it is taken pursuant to the state's common-law policy. Nor is the Amendment ineffective simply because the particular pattern of discrimination, which the State has enforced, was defined initially by the terms of a private agreement. State action, as that phrase is understood for the purposes of the Fourteenth Amendment, refers to exertions of state power in all forms. And when the effect of that action is to deny rights subject to the protection of the Fourteenth Amendment, it is the obligation of this Court to enforce the constitutional commands.

[13] We hold that in granting judicial enforcement of the restrictive agreements in these cases, the States have denied petitioners the equal protection of the laws and that, therefore, the action of the state courts cannot stand. We have noted that freedom from discrimination by the States in the enjoyment of property rights was among the basic objectives sought to be effectuated by the framers of the Fourteenth Amendment. That such discrimination has occurred in these cases is clear. Because of the race or color of these petitioners they have been denied rights of ownership or occupancy enjoyed as a matter of course by other citizens of different race or color. The Fourteenth Amendment declares "that all persons, whether colored or white, shall stand equal before the laws of the States, and, in regard to the colored race, for whose protection the amendment was primarily designed, that no discrimination shall be made against them by law because of their color." Strauder v. West Virginia, supra, 100 U.S. at 307, 25 L.Ed. 664. Only recently this Court has had occasion to declare that a

state law which denied equal enjoyment of property rights to a designated class of citizens of specified race and ancestry, was not a legitimate exercise of the state's police power but violated the guaranty of the equal protection of the laws. Oyama v. California, 1948, 332 U.S. 633, 68 S.Ct. 269. Nor may the discriminations imposed by the state courts in these cases be justified as proper exertions of state police power. Cf. Buchanan v. Warley, supra.

[14-16] Respondents urge, however, that since the state courts stand ready to enforce restrictive covenants excluding white persons from the ownership or occupancy of property covered by such agreements, enforcement of covenants excluding colored persons may not be deemed a denial of equal protection of the laws to the colored persons who are thereby affected. This contention does not bear scrutiny. The parties have directed our attention to no case in which a court, state or federal, has been called upon to enforce a covenant excluding members of the white majority from ownership or occupancy of real property on grounds of race or color. But there are more fundamental considerations. The rights created by the first section of the Fourteenth Amendment are, by its terms, guaranteed to the individual. The rights established are personal rights. It is, therefore, no answer to these petitioners to say that the courts may also be induced to deny white persons rights of ownership and occupancy on grounds of race or color. Equal protection of the laws is not achieved through indiscriminate imposition of inequalities.

[17, 18] Nor do we find merit in the suggestion that property owners who are parties to these agreements are denied equal protection of the laws if denied access to the courts to enforce the terms of restrictive covenants and to assert property rights which the state courts have held to be created by such agreements. The Constitution confers upon no individual the right to demand action by the State which results in the denial of equal protection of the laws to other individuals. And it would appear beyond question that the power of the State

to create and enforce property interests must be exercised within the boundaries defined by the Fourteenth Amendment. Cf. Marsh v. Alabama, 1946, 326 U.S. 501, 66 S.Ct. 276, 90 L.Ed. 265.

[19] The problem of defining the scope of the restrictions which the Federal Constitution imposes upon exertions of power by the States has given rise to many of the most persistent and fundamental issues which this Court has been called upon to consider. That problem was foremost in the minds of the framers of the Constitution, and since that early day, has arisen in a multitude of forms. The task of determining whether the action of a State offends constitutional provisions is one which may not be undertaken lightly. Where, however, it is clear that the action of the State violates the terms of the fundamental charter, it is the obligation of this Court so to declare.

[20] The historical context in which the Fourteenth Amendment became a part of the Constitution should not be forgotten. Whatever else the framers sought to achieve, it is clear that the matter of primary concern was the establishment of equality in the enjoyment of basic civil and political rights and the preservation of those rights from discriminatory action on the part of the States based on considerations of race or color. Seventy-five years ago this Court announced that the provisions of the Amendment are to be construed with this fundamental purpose in mind. Upon full consideration, we have concluded that in these cases the States have acted to deny petitioners the equal protection of the laws guaranteed by the Fourteenth Amendment. Having so decided, we find it unnecessary to consider whether petitioners have also been deprived of property without due process of law or denied privileges and immunities of citizens of the United States.

For the reasons stated, the judgment of the Supreme Court of Missouri and the judgment of the Supreme Court of Michigan must be reversed.

Reversed.

Mr. Justice Reed, Mr. Justice Jackson, and Mr. Justice Rutledge took no part in the consideration or decision of these cases.

May 3, 1948

4. From the Shadow of States' Rights

Hubert H. Humphrey Calls for a Strong Civil Rights Plank in the Platform of the Democratic National Convention—1948

It would ruin the party, it did not have a chance—but the young and idealistic civil rights advocates at the 1948 Democratic Convention held in Philadelphia were determined. They would write the recommendations of the President's Committee on Civil Rights into the party's platform; they would commend President Truman "for his courageous stand on the issue"; delegate Hubert H. Humphrey, Mayor of Minneapolis, would speak for the civil rights plank.

Humphrey was told that it was political madness, that he would kill his own future. Less than ten hours before the minority report was due to be made, Humphrey went to work on his speech.

By morning, the "idealists" were joined by a powerful Northern element of the party. Concerned about the Democrats' prospects in the upcoming elections, they recognized the potential of the civil rights issue among big city voters. One by one, delegations from Northern states agreed to support a strong civil rights position. The plank that was hopeless only a few hours before, now had a chance. In order to win adoption by the convention, it needed 617 votes—a majority.

Humphrey alternated between polishing his speech and button-holing delegates in the hotel's corridors to urge support. That afternoon the question of the civil rights plank was taken up at the convention. Chairman Sam Rayburn recognized the platform chairman who offered the moderate, majority-sponsored plank. The Alabama Governor spoke next—for a states' rights plank. Now it was the liberals' turn. After the minority report was read, Humphrey stepped forward to deliver his speech. It was short, direct, and earnest. Called by some "the greatest and most effective speech in politics," it was interrupted more than twenty times by applause—and a scattering of boos.

The speech was over in less than ten minutes. Minnesota and California delegates were the first to stand up and cheer. The Illinois delegation moved to the aisle to lead a parade. The standards of Minnesota, California, Wisconsin, Indiana, Connecticut, North Dakota, Kansas, West Virginia, Vermont, bobbed and weaved in the convention hall for a full eight minutes—nearly as long as it had taken Humphrey to deliver the speech.

When the final vote was announced, the liberal plank had won—651½ for, 582½ against. The convention recessed. Nearly three hours later, as Rayburn ordered the roll call for the Presidential nomination, thirty-five Southern delegates walked out of the hall. They were to form their own States' Rights Party—the "Dixiecrats"—with South Carolina Governor J. Strom Thurmond the candidate for President.

President Truman won the nomination of the Democratic Party and went on to an upset victory at the polls over Thomas E. Dewey. Henry Wallace and J. Strom Thurmond were also-rans.

Humphrey returned to Minneapolis, campaigned on his liberal record (he had also, as Mayor, established the first municipal Fair Employment Practices Commission), and won his first seat in the Senate.

The civil rights issue had not ruined either the Democratic Party or the men who had spoken up for it. And those who believed in equal rights breathed deeply of a new, fresh wind blowing over the nation.

SPEECH BY HUBERT H. HUMPHREY BEFORE THE DEMOCRATIC NATIONAL CONVENTION, JULY 14, 1948

I realize that I am dealing with a charged issue—with an issue which has been confused by emotionalism on all sides. I realize that there are those here—friends and colleagues of mine, many of them—who feel as deeply as I do about this issue and who are yet in complete disagreement with me.

My respect and admiration for these men and their views was great when I came here.

It is now far greater because of the sincerity, the courtesy, and the forthrightness with which they have argued in their discussions.

Because of this very respect—because of my profound belief that we have a challenging task to do here—because good conscience demands it—I feel I must rise at this time to support this report—a report that spells out our democracy, a report that the people will understand and enthusiastically acclaim.

Let me say at the outset that this proposal is made with no single region, no single class, no single racial or religious group in mind.

All regions and all states have shared in the precious heritage of American freedom. All states and all regions have at least some infringements on that freedom—all people, all groups have been the victims of discrimination.

The masterly statement of our keynote speaker, the distinguished United States Senator from Kentucky, Alben Barkley, made that point with great force. Speaking of the founder of our party, Thomas Jefferson, he said:

> He did not proclaim that all white, or black, or red, or yellow men are equal; that all Christian or Jewish men are equal; that all Protestant and Catholic men are equal; that all rich or poor men are equal; that all good or bad men are equal.
>
> What he declared was that all men are equal, and the equality which he proclaimed was equality in the right to enjoy the bless-

ings of free government in which they may participate and to
which they have given their consent.

We are here as Democrats. But more important, as Americans—and I firmly believe that as men concerned with our
country's future we must specify in our platform the guarantee which I have mentioned.

Yes, this is far more than a party matter. Every citizen has a
stake in the emergence of the United States as the leader of the
free world. That world is being challenged by the world of
slavery. For us to play our part effectively we must be in a
morally sound position.

We cannot use a double standard for measuring our own and
other people's policies. Our demands for democratic practices
in other lands will be no more effective than the guarantees of
those practiced in our own country.

We are God-fearing men and women. We place our faith in
the brotherhood of man under the fatherhood of God.

I do not believe that there can be any compromise on the
guarantee of civil rights which I have mentioned.

In spite of my desire for unanimous agreement on the platform there are some matters which I think must be stated without qualification. There can be no hedging—no watering
down.

There are those who say to you—we are rushing this issue of
civil rights. I say we are 172 years late.

There are those who say—this issue of civil rights is an in-
fringement on states' rights. The time has arrived for the Democratic Party to get out of the shadow of states' rights and
walk forthrightly into the bright sunshine of human rights.

People—human beings—this is the issue of the twentieth
century. People—all kinds and sorts of people—look to America for leadership—for help—for guidance.

My friends—my fellow Democrats—I ask you for a calm
consideration of our historic opportunity. Let us forget the
evil passions, the blindness of the past. In these times of world
economic, political, and spiritual—above all, spiritual—crisis,

we cannot—we must not, turn from the path so plainly before us.

That path has already led us through many valleys of the shadow of death. Now is the time to recall those who were left on that path of American freedom.

For all of us here, for the millions who have sent us, for the whole 2 billion members of the human family—our land is now, more than ever, the last best hope on earth. I know that we can—I know that we shall—begin here the fuller and richer realization of that hope—that promise of a land where all men are free and equal, and each man uses his freedom wisely and well.

5. Equality of Opportunity in the Armed Forces

A Presidential Order Heralds a Great Experiment in Democracy—1948

On July 26, 1948, President Truman issued two precedent-breaking executive orders. One instituted fair employment practices within the Federal Government's civilian agencies; the other ordered "equality of treatment and opportunity in the armed forces without regard to race, color, religion, or national origin."

Some persons credited Mr. Truman with doing more in one day for the cause of civil rights and equality than had been done in almost a century—and with doing it to prove he meant business. Others praised the President's accomplishment but claimed his action was forced upon him. After all, they pointed out, he was in the midst of a difficult Presidential election campaign and needed Northern urban votes.

Negro leaders used the situation to renew a campaign begun in 1940 and dropped after Pearl Harbor in the interest of a unified war effort. Mr. Truman, they said, reacted to pressure.

In the spring of 1948, A. Philip Randolph, chairman of a newly created League for Non-Violent Civil Disobedience Against Military Segregation, had threatened organized non-compliance with the military draft "unless President Truman issues an executive order against segregation." To a Congressional committee, Randolph said "I personally pledge myself to openly counsel, aid and abet youth, both white and Negro . . . in an organized refusal to register and be drafted." A poll conducted by the National Association for the Advancement of Colored People among draft-eligible Negro students found that 71 per cent were willing to go along with the civil disobedience campaign. But whether President Truman did indeed yield to the combined pressures of Negro leaders and politics, or whether he acted out of strong conviction, he nevertheless played a decisive role in breaking traditional patterns of discrimination.

Executive Order 9980 created a Fair Employment Board within the Civil Service Commission, ordered that only considerations of "merit and fitness" were valid in appointing and promoting personnel, established a departmental program to prevent discrimination, and appointed a fair employment officer to carry out the program.

Executive Order 9981 gave Jim Crow a dishonorable discharge. It was also to bring about a great experiment in practical integration, on the job, in schools, and in everyday living.

Before World War II ended, there were 1 million Negro servicemen, most confined to menial or construction work, or to a few all-Negro fighting units. In 1941, an Army spokesman had excused Jim Crow in uniform with these words: "The Army did not create the problem. . . . The Army is not a sociological laboratory; to be effective it must be organized and trained according to principles which will insure success."

It took seven years, under Presidents Truman and Eisenhower, to implement fully Executive Order 9981. In the process the armed forces became a "sociological laboratory" with millions of Americans—servicemen, civilians, and dependents —subject to integration in their daily lives. And it worked. Personal contact on an equal basis lowered the bars of prejudice. It did not, however, lead to forced social mixing, interracial marriages, or "mongrelization of the races." Furthermore, according to Army-sponsored studies made during the Korean War, nine out of ten white officers in Korea rated integrated units equal to or better than all-white units in morale, courage, and teamwork in combat.

If integration worked in the armed forces, why not in civilian life? The President's order was one more step forward, for its successful implementation brought new hope and impetus.

EXECUTIVE ORDER 9981

ESTABLISHING THE PRESIDENT'S COMMITTEE ON EQUALITY OF TREATMENT AND OPPORTUNITY IN THE ARMED FORCES

Whereas it is essential that there be maintained in the armed services of the United States the highest standards of democracy, with equality of treatment and opportunity for all those who serve in our country's defense:

Now, therefore, by virtue of the authority vested in me as President of the United States, by the Constitution and the statutes of the United States, and as Commander in Chief of the armed services, it is hereby ordered as follows:

1. It is hereby declared to be the policy of the President that there shall be equality of treatment and opportunity for all persons in the armed forces without regard to race, color, religion, or national origin. This policy shall be put into effect as rapidly as possible, having due regard to the time required to effectuate any necessary changes without impairing efficiency or morale.

2. There shall be created in the National Military Establishment an advisory committee to be known as the President's Committee on Equality of Treatment and Opportunity in the Armed Services, which shall be composed of seven members to be designated by the President.

3. The Committee is authorized on behalf of the President to examine into the rules, procedures, and practices of the armed services in order to determine in what respect such rules, procedures, and practices may be altered or improved with a view to carrying out the policy of this order. The Committee shall confer and advise with the Secretary of Defense, the Secretary of the Army, the Secretary of the Navy, and the Secretary of the Air Force, and shall make such recommendations to the President and to said Secretaries as in the judgment of the Committee will effectuate the policy hereof.

4. All executive departments and agencies of the Federal

Government are authorized and directed to cooperate with the Committee in its work, and to furnish the Committee such information or the services of such persons as the Committee may require in the performance of its duties.

5. When requested by the Committee to do so, persons in the armed services or in any of the executive departments and agencies of the Federal Government shall testify before the Committee and shall make available for the use of the Committee such documents and other information as the Committee may require.

6. The Committee shall continue to exist until such time as the President shall terminate its existence by Executive order.

HARRY S. TRUMAN

THE WHITE HOUSE
July 26, 1948

6. New Start for an Old Idea

The Supreme Court Upholds a Seventy-five-Year-Old Statute Prohibiting Segregation in Washington, D.C.—1953

A free American Negro, Benjamin Banneker, served on the commission which first surveyed and laid out Washington, D.C. Banneker, a mathematician, naturalist, and philosopher who was appointed to the commission by President Washington, would have found life difficult in nineteenth- and twentieth-century Washington.

The rules of segregation were strict and unyielding in the nation's capital. Hotels, theaters, movie houses, restaurants all closed their doors to Negroes. Downtown lunch counters, which did serve Negroes, expected them to eat standing up. White cab drivers would not bother to stop for Negro fares; white clerks in the "best" department stores turned their backs.

Henry Clay had called nineteenth-century Jim Crow in Washington a "blot on our nation." In 1947, President Truman's Committee on Civil Rights described the treatment of Negroes in Washington as shameful, absurd, and intolerable. It recommended enactment by Congress of legislation to eliminate discrimination and segregation in the District. None was forthcoming.

On June 8, 1953, the Supreme Court ruled that public eating places in the District of Columbia could not refuse service because of race or color. Subsequently, the District Board of Commissioners announced that it intended to enforce nondiscrimination not only with respect to restaurants, but to other places of public accommodation—including hotels, barber shops, bathing houses, and places of public amusement.

The irony was that Washington, D.C., had had a statute prohibiting racial segregation all along. The Supreme Court had upheld a local law that had not been enforced for more than seventy-five years.

In 1872, the Legislative Assembly of the District of Columbia passed an act prohibiting the keepers or proprietors of restaurants, hotels, "ice-cream saloons, or places where soda-water is kept for sale," barber shops, and bathing houses from "refusing to sell or wait upon any respectable well-behaved person without regard to race, color, or previous condition of servitude." In 1873, the Legislative Assembly passed another act, as direct in meaning, but specifically applicable only to "restaurants, eating houses, bar-rooms, sample rooms, ice-cream saloons, and soda-fountain rooms."

Now, eighty years later, the Supreme Court, in the case of *District of Columbia* v. *John R. Thompson Co., Inc.,* held that both acts had "survived the intervening changes in the government of the District of Columbia and are presently enforceable."

Almost overnight, restaurants, then hotels, movies, public pools, and bowling alleys were desegregated. One year later the Supreme Court was to order desegregation of the nation's schools, and in a separate decision handed down at the same time, remove the color bar from District of Columbia schools as well.

In the nation's capital, the hub of world democracy, the pattern of segregation was, at last, legally destroyed.

DISTRICT OF COLUMBIA v. JOHN R. THOMPSON CO., INC.

Mr. Justice Douglas delivered the opinion of the Court.

This is a criminal proceeding prosecuted by information against respondent for refusal to serve certain members of the Negro race at one of its restaurants in the District of Columbia solely on account of the race and color of those persons. The information is in four counts, the first charging a violation of the Act of the Legislative Assembly of the District of Columbia, June 20, 1872, and the others charging violations of the Act of the Legislative Assembly of the District of Columbia, June 26, 1873, L.Dist.Col.1871-1873, pp. 65, 116. Each Act makes it a crime to discriminate against a person on account of race or color or to refuse service to him on that ground.

The Municipal Court quashed the information on the ground that the 1872 and 1873 Acts had been repealed by implication on the enactment by Congress of the Organic Act of June 11, 1878, 20 Stat. 102. On appeal the Municipal Court of Appeals held that the 1872 and 1873 Acts were valid when enacted, that the former Act insofar as it applies to restaurants, had been repealed, but that the latter Act was still in effect. It therefore affirmed the Municipal Court insofar as it dismissed the count based on the 1872 Act and reversed the Municipal Court on the other counts. 81 A.2d 249. On cross-appeal, the Court of Appeals held that the 1872 and 1873 Acts were unenforceable and that the entire information should be dismissed. 92 U.S. App.D.C. —, 203 F.2d 579. The case is here on certiorari.

I

The history of congressional legislation dealing with the District of Columbia begins with the Act of July 16, 1790, 1 Stat. 130, by which the District was established as the permanent seat of the Government of the United States. We need not review for the purposes of this case the variety of congressional enactments pertaining to the management of the affairs of the District between that date and 1871. It is with the Organic Act of February 21, 1871, 16 Stat. 419, that we are particularly concerned.

That Act created a government by the name of the District of Columbia, constituted it "a body corporate for municipal purposes" with all of the powers of a municipal corporation "not inconsistent with the Constitution and laws of the United States and the provisions of this act," and gave it jurisdiction over all the territory within the limits of the District. §1. The Act vested "legislative power and authority" in a Legislative Assembly consisting of a Council and a House of Delegates, members of the Council to be appointed by the President with the advice and consent of the Senate and members of the House of Delegates to be elected by male citizens residing in the District. §§5, 7. The act provided, with exceptions not material here, that "the legislative power of the District shall extend to all rightful subjects of legislation within said District, consistent with the Constitution of the United States and the provisions of this act." §18. All acts of the Legislative Assembly were made subject at all times "to repeal or modification" by Congress. §18. And it was provided that nothing in the Act should be construed to deprive Congress of "the power of legislation" over the District "in as ample manner as if this law had not been enacted." §18. Executive power was vested in a governor appointed by the President by and with the advice of the Senate. §2. And it was provided that the District should have in the House of Representatives an elected delegate having the same rights and privileges as those of delegates from federal territories. §34.

This government (which was short-lived) was characterized by the Court as a "territorial government." Eckloff v. District of Columbia, 135 U.S. 240, 241, 10 S.Ct. 752, 34 L.Ed. 120. The analogy is an apt one. The grant to the Legislative Assembly by §18 of legislative power which extends "to all rightful subjects of legislation" is substantially identical with the grant of legislative power to territorial governments which reads: "The legislative power of every Territory shall extend to all rightful subjects of legislation not inconsistent with the Constitution and laws of the United States." R.S. §1851.

The power of Congress over the District and its power over the Territories are phrased in very similar language in the Constitution. Article I, §8, cl. 17 of the Constitution provides that "The Congress shall have Power * * * To exercise exclusive Legislation in all Cases whatsoever, over such District (not exceeding ten Miles square) as may, by Cession of particular States, and the Acceptance of Congress, become the Seat of the Government of the United States." Article IV, §3, cl. 2 of the Constitution grants Congress authority over territories in the following words:

> "The Congress shall have Power to dispose of and make all needful Rules and Regulations respecting the Territory or other Property belonging to the United States * * *."

. . . .

[6, 7] We conclude that the Congress had the authority under Art. I, §8, cl. 17 of the Constitution to delegate its lawmaking authority to the Legislative Assembly of the municipal corporation which was created by the Organic Act of 1871 and that the "rightful subjects of legislation" within the meaning of §18 of that Act was as broad as the police power of a state so as to include a law prohibiting discriminations against Negroes by the owners and managers of restaurants in the District of Columbia.

II

[8-10] The Acts of 1872 and 1873 survived, we think, all subsequent changes in the government of the District of Columbia and remain today a part of the governing body of laws applicable to the District. The Legislative Assembly was abolished by the Act of June 20, 1874, 18 Stat. 116. That Act provided that the District should be governed by a Commission.

§2. The Revised Statutes relating to the District of Columbia, approved June 20, 1874, kept in full force the prior laws and ordinances "not inconsistent with this chapter, and except as modified or repealed by Congress or the legislative assembly of the District." §91. Those Acts were followed by the present Organic Act of the District of Columbia approved June 11, 1878, 20 Stat. 102, which provides that "all laws now in force relating to the District of Columbia not inconsistent with the provisions of this act shall remain in full force and effect." §1. We find nothing in the 1874 Act nor in the 1878 Act inconsistent with the Acts here in question. And we find no other intervening act which would effect a repeal of them. Nor is there any suggestion in the briefs or oral argument that the Acts of 1872 and 1873, presently litigated, did not survive the Acts of 1874 and 1878. It indeed appears the Acts of 1874 and 1878 precluded the repeal of these anti-discrimination laws except by an Act of Congress. As Metropolitan R. Co. v. District of Columbia, supra, 132 U.S. at page 7, 10 S.Ct. at page 22 says the "legislative powers" of the District ceased with the Organic Act and thereafter municipal government was confined "to mere administration."

The Commissioners by the Joint Resolution of February 26, 1892, 27 Stat. 394, were vested with local legislative power as respects "reasonable and usual police regulations." But there is no suggestion that their power to make local ordinances was ever exercised to supplant these anti-discrimination laws of the Legislative Assembly with new and different ordinances. Rather the argument is that the 1872 and 1873 Acts were repealed by the Code of 1901, 31 Stat. 1189. Section 1636 of that Code provides in part:

"All acts and parts of acts of the general assembly of the State of Maryland general and permanent in their nature, all like acts and parts of acts of the legislative assembly of the District of Columbia, and all like acts and parts of acts of Congress applying solely to the District of Columbia in force in said District on the day of the passage of this act are hereby repealed, except: * * * .

"Third. Acts and parts of acts relating to the organization of the District government, or to its obligations, or the powers or duties of the Commissioners of the District of Columbia, or their subordinates or employees, or to police regulations, and generally all acts and parts of acts relating to municipal affairs only, including those regulating the charges of public-service corporations. * * * "

[11, 12] The Court of Appeals held that these anti-discrimination laws were "general and permanent" legislation within the meaning of §1636 and repealed by it, not being saved by the exceptions. The Department of Justice presents an elaborate argument, based on the legislative history of the 1901 Code, to the effect that the anti-discrimination laws here involved were not "general and permanent" laws within the meaning of §1636. But the lines of analysis presented are quite shadowy; and we find it difficult not to agree that the 1872 and 1873 Acts were "general and permanent" as contrasted to statutes which are private, special, or temporary. That is the sense in which we believe the words "general and permanent" were used in the Code. We conclude, however, that they were saved from repeal by the *Third* exception clause quoted above.

It is our view that these anti-discrimination laws governing restaurants in the District are "police regulations" and acts "relating to municipal affairs" within the meaning of the *Third* exception in §1636. The Court of Appeals in United States v. Cella, 37 App.D.C. 433, 435, in construing an Act providing that prosecutions for violations of penal statutes "in the nature of police or municipal regulations" should be in the name of the District, said,

"A municipal ordinance or police regulation is peculiarly applicable to the inhabitants of a particular place; in other words, it is local in character."

The laws which require equal service to all who eat in restaurants in the District are as local in character as laws regulating public health, schools, streets, and parks. In Johnson v. District of Columbia, 30 App.D.C. 520, the Court of Appeals held that an Act of the Legislative Assembly prohibiting cruelty to animals was a police regulation saved from repeal by the *Third* exception to § 1636. The court said it was legislation "in the interest of peace and order" and conducive "to the morals and general welfare of the community." 30 App.D.C. at page 522. Regulation of public eating and drinking establishments in the District has been delegated by Congress to the municipal government from the very beginning. In terms of the history of the District of Columbia there is indeed no subject of legislation more firmly identified with local affairs than the regulation of restaurants.

[13-15] There remains for consideration only whether the Acts of 1872 and 1873 were abandoned or repealed as a result of non-use and administrative practice. There was one view in the Court of Appeals that these laws are presently unenforceable for that reason. We do not agree. The failure of the executive branch to enforce a law does not result in its modification or repeal. See Louisville & N. R. Co. v. United States, 282 U.S. 740, 759, 51 S.Ct. 297, 304, 75 L.Ed. 672; United States v. Morton Salt Co., 338 U.S. 632, 647, 648, 70 S.Ct. 357, 366, 94 L.Ed. 401. The repeal of laws is as much a legislative function as their enactment.

Congress has had the power to repeal the 1872 and 1873 Acts from the dates of their passage by the Legislative Assembly. But as we have seen, it has not done so.

Congress also has had the authority to delegate to a municipal government for the District the power to pass laws which would alter or repeal the Acts of the Legislative Assembly. As we have seen, the Organic Act of the District of Columbia approved June 11, 1878, withdrew legislative powers from the municipal government. In 1892 the Commissioners were given legislative power as respects "reasonable and usual police regulations." That legislative authority could have been employed to repeal the Acts of 1872 and 1873. See Stevens v. Stoutenburgh, 8 App.D.C. 513. For as we have noted, regulations of restaurants is a matter plainly within the scope of police regulation. But the Commissioners passed no ordinances dealing with the rights of Negroes in the restaurants of the District. It is argued that their power to do so was withdrawn by Congress in the Code of 1901. It is pointed out that the Code of 1901 kept in force the acts, ordinances, and regulations not repealed; and from that the conclusion is drawn that only Congress could thereafter amend or repeal these enactments of the Legislative Assembly.

We find it unnecessary to resolve that question. For even if we assume that after the Code of 1901 the Commissioners had the authority to replace these anti-discrimination laws with other ones, we find no indication that they ever did so. Certainly no ordinance was enacted which purported to repeal or modify those laws or which, by providing a different measure of a restaurant owner's duty, established a standard in conflict with that provided by the Legislative Assembly.

But it is said that the licensing authority of the Commissioners over restaurants has been employed for 75 years without regard to the equal service requirements of the 1872 and 1873 Acts, that no licenses have been forfeited for violations of those Acts, and that the licensing authority of the Commissioners has been employed in effect to repeal or set aside the provisions of those Acts. But those regulations are health, safety, and sanitary measures. They do not purport to be a complete codification of ordinances regulating restaurants. They contain neither a requirement that Negroes be segregated nor that Negroes be treated without discrimination. The case therefore appears to us no different than one where the executive department neglects or refuses to enforce a requirement long prescribed by the legislature.

It would be a more troublesome case if the 1872 and 1873 Acts were licensing laws which through the years had been modified and changed under the legislative authority of the Commissioners. But these Acts do not provide any machinery for the granting and revocation of licenses. They are *regulatory* laws prescribing in terms of civil rights the duties of restaurant owners to members of the public. Upon conviction for violating their provisions, penalties are imposed. There is a fine and in addition a forfeiture of license without right of renewal for a year. But these Acts, unlike the sanitary requirements laid upon restaurants, do not prescribe conditions for the issuance of a license. Like the regulation of wages and hours of work, the employment of minors, and the requirement that restaurants have flameproof draperies, these laws merely *regulate* a licensed business. Therefore, the exercise of the *licensing* authority of the Commissioners could not modify, alter, or repeal these laws. Nor can we discover any other legislative force which has removed them from the existing body of law.

[16] Cases of hardship are put where criminal laws so long in disuse as to be no longer known to exist are enforced against innocent parties. But that condition does not bear on the continuing validity of the law; it is only an ameliorating factor in enforcement.

We have said that the Acts of 1872 and 1873 survived the intervening changes in the government of the District of Columbia and are presently enforceable. We would speak more accurately if we said that the 1873 Act survived. For there is a subsidiary question, which we do not reach and which will be open on remand of the cause to the Court of Appeals, whether the 1872 Act under which the first count of the information is laid was repealed by the 1873 Act. On that we express no opinion.

Reversed.

Mr. Justice Jackson took no part in the consideration or decision of this case.

June 8, 1953

7. To the Heart of the Matter

*The Supreme Court Decides that the Doctrine of
"Separate but Equal" Has No Place in Public
Education—1954*

The fight for equality was moving ahead, step by step. On every front, patterns of discrimination were being torn—but not destroyed. There was still no major victory, no spectacular advance. The time had come for the major advance.

Where? To the heart of the matter, civil rights proponents said: education.

The concerted campaign began in 1950. There had been skirmishes and victories before—at the highest levels of education, a Negro here and there admitted to a graduate school when it was proven that there was no "separate but equal" facility available. Now Thurgood Marshall, as chief counsel for the National Association for the Advancement of Colored People, mobilized a different kind of attack—against "separate but equal" itself, the *Plessy* v. *Ferguson* decision of 1896—an attack against the entire system from elementary school up. The groundwork was prepared for Supreme Court appeals that were to end in victory. In meeting after meeting sponsored by the NAACP and convened by Marshall, lawyers, sociologists, psychiatrists, and educators prepared the arguments to be put before the Court.

In 1953, four cases en bloc reached the high tribunal—appealed from courts in Kansas, South Carolina, Virginia and Delaware. Each was slightly different but all asked the Court to decide one basic question: "Does segregation of children in public schools solely on the basis of race, even though the physical facilities and other tangible factors may be equal, deprive the children of the minority group of equal educational opportunities?" The Court's answer, on May 17, 1954, was: Yes.

Although it suspended any action on the ruling for a year in

order to examine means of effective implementation, this was
the most spectacular advance yet. The Supreme Court had
thrown out "separate but equal," the legal shelter for racial
segregation. All state laws authorizing or requiring segregation
in public schools had lost their constitutional validity.

On May 31, 1955, the Supreme Court gave its order implementing the decision. Conscious of the problems desegregation
would produce, it directed lower federal courts to issue "with
all deliberate speed" the necessary orders to admit students to
public schools on a racially nondiscriminatory basis.

In communities throughout the South, Negro students were
to become pioneers of democracy. And white Americans
throughout the nation, looking in disbelief at photographs of
jeering, stone-throwing mobs shrieking their hate at Negro
children, were about to become "involved"—to understand
and sympathize with the Negro's plight, perhaps for the first
time.

Peaceful but token transitions in Atlanta, Dallas, New Or-
leans, and Memphis were countered by the violence of Little
Rock, the attempted circumvention of law in Prince Edward
County where public schools were closed for four years rather
than yield to integration, the bombing of a school in Nashville
which one small Negro child had desegregated the day before.

But with each incident of violence, each hastily enacted, and
illegal statute, to evade desegregation, the importance of the
Supreme Court decision became increasingly clear. Despite the
slowness of "all deliberate speed," the defenders of white supremacy had been put on the defensive. They could delay,
they could protest, but that was all they could do. The Negro
had won his biggest battle.

BROWN v. BOARD OF EDUCATION

Mr. Chief Justice Warren delivered the opinion of the Court.

These cases come to us from the States of Kansas, South Carolina, Virginia, and Delaware. They are premised on different facts and different local conditions, but a common legal question justifies their consideration together in this consolidated opinion.

In each of the cases, minors of the Negro race, through their legal representatives, seek the aid of the courts in obtaining admission to the public schools of their community on a nonsegregated basis. In each instance, they had been denied admission to schools attended by white children under laws requiring or permitting segregation according to race. This segregation was alleged to deprive the plaintiffs of the equal protection of the laws under the Fourteenth Amendment. In each of the cases other than the Delaware case, a three-judge federal district court denied relief to the plaintiffs on the so-called "separate but equal" doctrine announced by this Court in *Plessy* v. *Ferguson*, 163 U.S. 537. Under that doctrine, equality of treatment is accorded when the races are provided substantially equal facilities, even though these facilities be separate. In the Delaware case, the Supreme Court of Delaware adhered to that doctrine, but ordered that the plaintiffs be admitted to the white schools because of their superiority to the Negro schools.

The plaintiffs contend that segregated public schools are not "equal" and cannot be made "equal," and that hence they are deprived of the equal protection of the laws. Because of the obvious importance of the question presented, the Court took jurisdiction. Argument was heard in the 1952 Term, and reargument was heard this Term on certain questions propounded by the Court.

Reargument was largely devoted to the circumstances surrounding the adoption of the Fourteenth Amendment in 1868.

It covered exhaustively consideration of the Amendment in Congress, ratification by the states, then existing practices in racial segregation, and the views of proponents and opponents of the Amendment. This discussion and our own investigation convince us that, although these sources cast some light, it is not enough to resolve the problem with which we are faced. At best, they are inconclusive. The most avid proponents of the post-War Amendments undoubtedly intended them to remove all legal distinctions among "all persons born or naturalized in the United States." Their opponents, just as certainly, were antagonistic to both the letter and the spirit of the Amendments and wished them to have the most limited effect. What others in Congress and the state legislatures had in mind cannot be determined with any degree of certainty.

An additional reason for the inconclusive nature of the Amendment's history, with respect to segregated schools, is the status of public education at that time. In the South, the movement toward free common schools, supported by general taxation, had not yet taken hold. Education of white children was largely in the hands of private groups. Education of Negroes was almost nonexistent, and practically all of the race were illiterate. In fact, any education of Negroes was forbidden by law in some states. Today, in contrast, many Negroes have achieved outstanding success in the arts and sciences as well as in the business and professional world. It is true that public education had already advanced further in the North, but the effect of the Amendment on Northern States was generally ignored in the congressional debates. Even in the North, the conditions of public education did not approximate those existing today. The curriculum was usually rudimentary; ungraded schools were common in rural areas; the school term was but three months a year in many states; and compulsory school attendance was virtually unknown. As a consequence, it is not surprising that there should be so little in the history of the Fourteenth Amendment relating to its intended effect on public education.

In the first cases in this Court construing the Fourteenth

Amendment, decided shortly after its adoption, the Court interpreted it as proscribing all state-imposed discriminations against the Negro race. The doctrine of "separate but equal" did not make its appearance in this Court until 1896 in the case of *Plessy* v. *Ferguson, supra,* involving not education but transportation. American courts have since labored with the doctrine for over half a century. In this Court, there have been six cases involving the "separate but equal" doctrine in the field of public education. In *Cumming* v. *County Board of Education,* 175 U.S. 528, and *Gong Lum* v. *Rice,* 275 U.S. 78, the validity of the doctrine itself was not challenged. In more recent cases, all on the graduate school level, inequality was found in that specific benefits enjoyed by white students were denied to Negro students of the same educational qualifications. *Missouri ex rel. Gaines* v. *Canada,* 305 U.S. 337; *Sipuel* v. *Oklahoma,* 332 U.S. 631; *Sweatt* v. *Painter,* 339 U.S. 629; *McLaurin* v. *Oklahoma State Regents,* 339 U.S. 637. In none of these cases was it necessary to re-examine the doctrine to grant relief to the Negro plaintiff. And in *Sweatt* v. *Painter, supra,* the Court expressly reserved decision on the question whether *Plessy* v. *Ferguson* should be held inapplicable to public education.

In the instant cases, that question is directly presented. Here, unlike *Sweatt* v. *Painter,* there are findings below that the Negro and white schools involved have been equalized, or are being equalized, with respect to buildings, curricula, qualifications and salaries of teachers, and other "tangible" factors. Our decision, therefore, cannot turn on merely a comparison of these tangible factors in the Negro and white schools involved in each of the cases. We must look instead to the effect of segregation itself on public education.

In approaching this problem, we cannot turn the clock back to 1868, when the Amendment was adopted, or even to 1896 when *Plessy* v. *Ferguson* was written. We must consider public education in the light of its full development and its present place in American life throughout the nation. Only in this way can it be determined if segregation in public schools deprives these plaintiffs of the equal protection of the laws.

Today, education is perhaps the most important function of state and local governments. Compulsory school attendance laws and the great expenditures for education both demonstrate our recognition of the importance of education to our democratic society. It is required in the performance of our most basic public responsibilities, even service in the armed forces. It is the very foundation of good citizenship. Today it is a principal instrument in awakening the child to cultural values, in preparing him for later professional training, and in helping him to adjust normally to his environment. In these days, it is doubtful that any child may reasonably be expected to succeed in life if he is denied the opportunity of an education. Such an opportunity, where the state has undertaken to provide it, is a right which must be made available to all on equal terms.

We come then to the question presented: Does segregation of children in public schools solely on the basis of race, even though the physical facilities and other "tangible" factors may be equal, deprive the children of the minority group of equal educational opportunities? We believe that it does.

In *Sweatt* v. *Painter, supra,* in finding that a segregated law school for Negroes could not provide them equal educational opportunities, this Court relied in large part on "those qualities which are incapable of objective measurement but which make for greatness in a law school." In *McLaurin* v. *Oklahoma State Regents, supra,* the Court, in requiring that a Negro admitted to a white graduate school be treated like all other students, again resorted to intangible considerations: ". . . his ability to study, to engage in discussions and exchange views with other students, and, in general, to learn his profession." Such considerations apply with added force to children in grade and high schools. To separate them from others of similar age and qualifications solely because of their race generates a feeling of inferiority as to their status in the community that may affect their hearts and minds in a way unlikely ever to be undone. The effect of this separation on their educational opportunities was well stated by a finding in the Kansas case by a court which nevertheless felt compelled to rule against the Negro plaintiffs:

> "Segregation of white and colored children in public schools has a detrimental effect upon the colored children. The impact is greater when it has the sanction of the law; for the policy of separating the races is usually interpreted as denoting the inferiority of the Negro group. A sense of inferiority affects the motivation of a child to learn. Segregation with the sanction of law, therefore, has a tendency to retard the educational and mental development of Negro children and to deprive them of some of the benefits they would receive in a racially integrated school system."

Whatever may have been the extent of psychological knowledge at the time of *Plessy* v. *Ferguson*, this finding is amply supported by modern authority. Any language in *Plessy* v. *Ferguson* contrary to this finding is rejected.

We conclude that in the field of public education the doctrine of "separate but equal" has no place. Separate educational facilities are inherently unequal. Therefore, we hold that the plaintiffs and others similarly situated for whom the actions have been brought are, by reason of the segregation complained of, deprived of the equal protection of the laws guaranteed by the Fourteenth Amendment. This disposition makes unnecessary any discussion whether such segregation also violates the Due Process Clause of the Fourteenth Amendment.

Because these are class actions, because of the wide applicability of this decision, and because of the great variety of local conditions, the formulation of decrees in these cases presents problems of considerable complexity. On reargument, the consideration of appropriate relief was necessarily subordinated to the primary question—the constitutionality of segregation in public education. We have now announced that such segregation is a denial of the equal protection of the laws. In order that we may have the full assistance of the parties in formulating decrees, the cases will be restored to the docket, and the parties are requested to present further argument on Questions 4 and 5 previously propounded by the Court for the reargument this Term. The Attorney General of the United States is again invited to participate. The Attorneys General of the states requiring or permitting segregation in public education will also be permitted to appear as *amici curiae* upon request to do so by September 15, 1954, and submission of briefs by October 1, 1954.

It is so ordered.

May 17, 1954

8. The First Federal Civil Rights Law Since Reconstruction

The Civil Rights Act of 1957

On September 9, 1957, President Dwight D. Eisenhower signed into law "an Act to provide means of further securing and protecting the civil rights of persons within the jurisdiction of the United States." Congress had finally responded to the new attitudes and hopes that had arisen throughout the nation. And the United States had its first new civil rights act in eighty-two years—since the days of Reconstruction.

The act came after long debate and maneuvering. A compromise between long-felt aspirations and deeply entrenched fears, it would not bring the millennium in America. Civil rights groups called it the "minimum meaningful bill they could accept." But it was an act. The fight for civil rights had moved to three fronts—the executive branch of government, the Supreme Court, and Congress.

Although the bill was passed after long Congressional debate, there were no racial slanders such as had marked civil rights discussions in the past, and there was no filibuster. The overwhelming re-election of President Eisenhower revealed a shift in Negro voting away from the Democratic Party. Many Republican politicians, previously lukewarm to the civil rights issue, saw continued Republican victories if Negro votes could be retained and increased. To Democrats, it was clear that the party's immobilization by Southern filibusters would prevent the recapture of national power. The bill was pushed on and passed by a coalition of Republicans and liberal Democrats.

The new civil rights law provided for:

—establishment of a special Civil Rights Division within the Department of Justice;

—creation of a Federal Civil Rights Commission to study the

status of civil rights in the nation and make recommendations for legislation. The Commission was armed with subpoena powers to compel witnesses to testify and produce records;

—authority for the Department of Justice to intervene, in the name of the United States, in behalf of individuals in instances of actual or threatened violations of general civil rights, such as the right to attend an integrated school;

—similar authorization for Federal intervention against violations of the right to vote.

The sole purpose of the Commission on Civil Rights, fact-finding and reporting, gave it a unique role—that of duly appointed conscience of the Federal Government. Its function was to look beyond individual complaints of racially motivated injustice, to determine whether effective remedies were available, and if they were not, to call the lack to the attention of the President and the Congress. In theory, if not always in practice, the next step would be legislation or executive action.

The Commission's reports, in 1959, and in 1961, during its second term, left no room for smugness. It recommended that Congress abolish literacy tests in all elections; that legislation be adopted requiring every local school board that still maintained segregated schools to file a desegregation plan within six months; that federal laws be enacted providing strengthened criminal sanctions against unlawful official violence and subjecting local governments to liability for unlawful acts of its officers. It also urged the President to take strong executive action in all fields. The 1961 report contained thirty-seven recommendations for legislative and executive action.

THE CIVIL RIGHTS ACT OF 1957

PART I—ESTABLISHMENT OF THE COMMISSION ON CIVIL RIGHTS

SEC. 101. (a) There is created in the executive branch of the Government a Commission on Civil Rights (hereinafter called the "Commission").

(b) The Commission shall be composed of six members who shall be appointed by the President by and with the advice and consent of the Senate. Not more than three of the members shall at any one time be of the same political party.

(c) The President shall designate one of the members of the Commission as Chairman and one as Vice Chairman. The Vice Chairman shall act as Chairman in the absence or disability of the Chairman, or in the event of a vacancy in that office.

(d) Any vacancy in the Commission shall not affect its powers and shall be filled in the same manner, and subject to the same limitation with respect to party affiliations as the original appointment was made.

(e) Four members of the Commission shall constitute a quorum.

RULES OF PROCEDURE OF THE COMMISSION

SEC. 102. (a) The Chairman or one designated by him to act as Chairman at a hearing of the Commission shall announce in an opening statement the subject of the hearing.

(b) A copy of the Commission's rules shall be made available to the witness before the Commission.

(c) Witnesses at the hearings may be accompanied by their own counsel for the purpose of advising them concerning their constitutional rights.

(d) The Chairman or Acting Chairman may punish breaches of order and decorum and unprofessional ethics on the part of counsel, by censure and exclusion from the hearings.

(e) If the Commission determines that evidence or testimony at any hearing may tend to defame, degrade, or incriminate any person, it shall (1) receive such evidence or testimony in executive session; (2) afford such person an opportunity voluntarily to appear as a witness; and (3) receive and dispose of requests from such person to subpoena additional witnesses.

(f) Except as provided in sections 102 and 105 (f) of this Act, the Chairman shall receive and the Commission shall dispose of requests to subpoena additional witnesses.

(g) No evidence or testimony taken in executive session may be released or used in public sessions without the consent of the Commission. Whoever releases or uses in public without the consent of the Commission evidence or testimony taken in executive session shall be fined not more than $1,000, or imprisoned for not more than one year.

(h) In the discretion of the Commission, witnesses may submit brief and pertinent sworn statements in writing for inclusion in the record. The Commission is the sole judge of the pertinency of testimony and evidence adduced at its hearings.

DUTIES OF THE COMMISSION

Sec. 104. (a) The Commission shall—

(1) investigate allegations in writing under oath or affirmation that certain citizens of the United States are being deprived of their right to vote and have that vote counted by reason of their color, race, religion, or national origin; which writing, under oath or affirmation, shall set forth the facts upon which such belief or beliefs are based;

(2) study and collect information concerning legal developments constituting a denial of equal protection of the laws under the Constitution; and

(3) appraise the laws and policies of the Federal Government with respect to equal protection of the laws under the Constitution.

(b) The Commission shall submit interim reports to the President and to the Congress at such times as either the Commission or the President shall deem desirable, and shall submit to the President and to the Congress a final and comprehensive report of its activities, findings, and recommendations not later than two years from the date of the enactment of this Act.

(c) Sixty days after the submission of its final report and recommendations the Commission shall cease to exist.

POWERS OF THE COMMISSION

SEC. 105. (a) There shall be a full-time staff director for the Commission who shall be appointed by the President by and with the advice and consent of the Senate and who shall receive compensation at a rate, to be fixed by the President, not in excess of $22,500 a year. The President shall consult with the Commission before submitting the nomination of any person for appointment to the position of staff director. Within the limitations of its appropriations, the Commission may appoint such other personnel as it deems advisable, in accordance with the civil service and classification laws, and may procure services as authorized by section 15 of the Act of August 2, 1946 (60 Stat. 810; 5 U. S. C. 55a), but at rates for individuals not in excess of $50 per diem.

(b) The Commission shall not accept or utilize services of voluntary or uncompensated personnel, and the term "whoever" as used in paragraph (g) and section 102 hereof shall be construed to mean a person whose services are compensated by the United States.

(c) The Commission may constitute such advisory committees within States composed of citizens of that State and may consult with governors, attorneys general, and other representatives of State and local governments, and private organizations, as it deems advisable.

(d) Members of the Commission, and members of advisory committees constituted pursuant to subsection (c) of this section, shall be exempt from the operations of sections 281, 283, 284, 434, and 1914 of title 18 of the United States Code, and section 190 of the Revised Statutes (5 U. S. C. 99).

(e) All Federal agencies shall cooperate fully with the Commission to the end that it may effectively carry out its functions and duties.

(f) The Commission, or on the authorization of the Commission any subcommittee of two or more members, at least one of whom shall be of each major political party, may, for the purpose of carrying out the provisions of this Act, hold such hearings and act at such times and places as the Commission or such authorized subcommittee may deem advisable. Subpoenas for the attendance and testimony of witnesses or the production of written or other matter may be issued in accordance with the rules of the Commission as contained in section 102 (j) and (k) of this Act, over the signature of the Chairman of the Commission or of such subcommittee, and may be served by any person designated by such Chairman.

(g) In case of contumacy or refusal to obey a subpoena, any district court of the United States or the United States court of any Territory or possession, or the District Court of the United States for the District of Columbia, within the jurisdiction of which the inquiry is carried on or within the jurisdiction of which said person guilty of contumacy or refusal to obey is found or resides or transacts business, upon application by the Attorney General of the United States shall have jurisdiction to issue to such person an order requiring such person to appear before the Commission or a subcommittee thereof, there to produce evidence if so ordered, or there to give testimony touching the matter under investigation; and any failure to obey such order of the court may be punished by said court as a contempt thereof.

APPROPRIATIONS

Sec. 106. There is hereby authorized to be appropriated, out of any money in the Treasury not otherwise appropriated, so much as may be necessary to carry out the provisions of this Act.

PART II—TO PROVIDE FOR AN ADDITIONAL ASSISTANT ATTORNEY GENERAL

SEC. 111. There shall be in the Department of Justice one additional Assistant Attorney General, who shall be appointed by the President, by and with the advice and consent of the Senate, who shall assist the Attorney General in the performance of his duties, and who shall receive compensation at the rate prescribed by law for other Assistant Attorneys General.

PART IV—TO PROVIDE MEANS OF FURTHER SECURING AND PROTECTING THE RIGHT TO VOTE

SEC. 131. Section 2004 of the Revised Statutes (42 U. S. C. 1971), is amended as follows:

(a) Amend the catch line of said section to read, "Voting rights."

(b) Designate its present text with the subsection symbol "(a)."

(c) Add, immediately following the present text, four new subsections to read as follows:

"(b) No person, whether acting under color of law or otherwise, shall intimidate, threaten, coerce, or attempt to intimidate, threaten, or coerce any other person for the purpose of interfering with the right of such other person to vote or to vote as he may choose, or of causing such other person to vote for, or not to vote for, any candidate for the office of President, Vice President, presidential elector, Member of the Senate, or Member of the House of Representatives, Delegates or Commissioners from the Territories or possessions, at any general, special, or primary election held solely or in part for the purpose of selecting or electing any such candidate.

"(c) Whenever any person has engaged or there are reasonable grounds to believe that any person is about to engage in any act or practice which would deprive any other person of any right or privilege secured by subsection (a) or (b), the Attorney General may institute for the United States, or in the name of the United States, a civil action or other proper proceeding for preventive relief, including an application for a permanent or temporary injunction, restraining order, or other order. In any proceeding hereunder the United States shall be liable for costs the same as a private person.

"(d) The district courts of the United States shall have jurisdiction of proceedings instituted pursuant to this section and shall exercise the same without regard to whether the party aggrieved shall have exhausted any administrative or other remedies that may be provided by law.

"(e) Any person cited for an alleged contempt under this Act shall be allowed to make his full defense by counsel learned in the law; and the court before which he is cited or tried, or some judge thereof, shall immediately, upon his request, assign to him such counsel, not exceeding two, as he may desire, who shall have free access to him at all reasonable hours. He shall be allowed, in his defense to make any proof that he can produce by lawful witnesses, and shall have the like process of the court to compel his witnesses to appear at his trial or hearing, as is usually granted to compel witnesses to appear on behalf of the prosecution. If such person shall be found by the court to be financially unable to provide for such counsel, it shall be the duty of the court to provide such counsel."

PART V—TO PROVIDE TRIAL BY JURY FOR PROCEEDINGS TO
PUNISH CRIMINAL CONTEMPTS OF COURT GROWING OUT
OF CIVIL RIGHTS CASES AND TO AMEND THE JUDICIAL
CODE RELATING TO FEDERAL JURY QUALIFICATIONS

SEC. 151. In all cases of criminal contempt arising under the provisions of this Act, the accused, upon conviction, shall be punished by fine or imprisonment or both: *Provided however,* That in case the accused is a natural person the fine to be paid shall not exceed the sum of $1,000, nor shall imprisonment exceed the term of six months: *Provided further,* That in any such proceeding for criminal contempt, at the discretion of the judge, the accused may be tried with or without a jury: *Provided further, however,* That in the event such proceeding for criminal contempt be tried before a judge without a jury and the sentence of the court upon conviction is a fine in excess of the sum of $300 or imprisonment in excess of forty-five days, the accused in said proceeding, upon demand therefor, shall be entitled to a trial de novo before a jury, which shall conform as near as may be to the practice in other criminal cases.

This section shall not apply to contempts committed in the presence of the court or so near thereto as to interfere directly with the administration of justice nor to the misbehavior, misconduct, or disobedience, of any officer of the court in respect to the writs, orders, or process of the court.

Nor shall anything herein or in any other provision of law be construed to deprive courts of their power, by civil contempt proceedings, without a jury, to secure compliance with or to prevent obstruction of, as distinguished from punishment for violations of, any lawful writ, process, order, rule, decree, or command of the court in accordance with the prevailing usages of law and equity, including the power of detention.

SEC. 152. Section 1861, title 28, of the United States Code is hereby amended to read as follows:

"§1861. Qualifications of Federal jurors

"Any citizen of the United States who has attained the age of twenty-one years and who has resided for a period of one year within the judicial district, is competent to serve as a grand or petit juror unless—

"(1) He has been convicted in a State or Federal court of record of a crime punishable by imprisonment for more than one year and his civil rights have not been restored by pardon or amnesty.

"(2) He is unable to read, write, speak, and understand the English language.

"(3) He is incapable, by reason of mental or physical infirmities to render efficient jury service."

SEC. 161. This Act may be cited as the "Civil Rights Act of 1957."

Approved September 9, 1957.

9. *The Ordeal of the American Negro*

From a Birmingham Jail, Martin Luther King, Jr., Defends Direct Action—1963

In 1955, an unknown young Baptist minister, Martin Luther King, Jr., found himself leading the historic Montgomery bus boycott. In 1956, the year-long boycott ended in victory when the Supreme Court ordered an end to segregated seating on public buses.

Four years later, a new mass movement began—sit-ins at segregated lunch counters. Chain stores with Jim Crow lunch counters in the South were picketed throughout the nation. "If a Negro dollar is good at the notions counter, it should be good at the lunch counter," signs and leaflets said. One large chain of stores reported an 18 per cent drop of sales during a three-month period. Four of America's leading variety stores integrated luncheon facilities in 112 Southern cities.

In 1961, the Congress of Racial Equality organized Freedom Rides aimed at desegregating interstate travel facilities. Attorney General Robert F. Kennedy asked the Interstate Commerce Commission to issue nationwide regulations banning segregation in interstate bus transportation and terminals, including waiting rooms, rest rooms, and restaurants.

In 1963, Martin Luther King, now well-known as the founder and president of the Southern Christian Leadership Conference, led "nonviolent direct action" demonstrations in Birmingham—the city, he said, with "more unsolved bombings of Negro homes and churches than any city in this nation." Dr. King was arrested for his efforts.

As the antisegregation demonstrations approached their climax, eight Alabama clergymen issued a public statement directed to King and calling the Negro protest actions "unwise and untimely": The statement said:

> We the undersigned clergymen are among those who, in January, issued "An Appeal for Law and Order and Common Sense," in dealing with racial problems in Alabama. We expressed understanding that honest convictions in racial matters could properly be pursued in the courts, but urged that decisions of those courts should in the meantime be peacefully obeyed.
>
> Since that time there had been some evidence of increased forbearance and a willingness to face facts. Responsible citizens have undertaken to work on various problems which cause racial friction and unrest. In Birmingham, recent public events have given indications that we all have opportunity for a new constructive and realistic approach to racial problems.
>
> However, we are now confronted by a series of demonstrations by some of our Negro citizens, directed and led in part by outsiders. We recognize the natural impatience of people who feel that their hopes are slow in being realized. But we are convinced that these demonstrations are unwise and untimely.
>
> We agree rather with certain local Negro leadership which has called for honest and open negotiation of racial issues in our area. And we believe this kind of facing of issues can best be accomplished by citizens of our own metropolitan area, white and Negro, meeting with their knowledge and experience of the local situation.

The statement went on to warn against actions that "incite to hatred and violence," to "commend the community as a whole, and the local news media and law enforcement officials in particular, on the calm manner in which these demonstrations have been handled," and to urge "our own Negro community to withdraw support from these demonstrations, and to unite locally in working peacefully for a better Birmingham."

The following month, Dr. King answered the statement from his cell in the Birmingham City Jail. He explained the steps in a nonviolent campaign, explained why he was in Birmingham—"because injustice is here"—and described, in simple and moving terms, the ordeal of the American Negro.

The Birmingham demonstrations presaged a national wave of protests. The Negro was using power, "pressure, more pressure, and still more pressure" to gain his Constitutional rights.

LETTER FROM BIRMINGHAM JAIL*

April 16, 1963

My Dear Fellow Clergymen:
While confined here in the Birmingham city jail, I came across your recent statement calling my present activities "unwise and untimely." Seldom do I pause to answer criticism of my work and ideas. If I sought to answer all the criticisms that cross my desk, my secretaries would have little time for anything other than such correspondence in the course of the day, and I would have no time for constructive work. But since I feel that you are men of genuine good will and that your criticisms are sincerely set forth, I want to try to answer your statement in what I hope will be patient and reasonable terms.

I think I should indicate why I am here in Birmingham, since you have been influenced by the view which argues against "outsiders coming in." I have the honor of serving as president of the Southern Christian Leadership Conference, an organization operating in every southern state, with headquarters in Atlanta, Georgia. We have some eighty-five affiliated organizations across the South, and one of them is the Alabama Christian Movement for Human Rights. Frequently we share staff, educational and financial resources with our affiliates. Several months ago the affiliate here in Birmingham asked us to be on call to engage in a nonviolent direct-action program if such were deemed necessary. We readily consented, and when the hour came we lived up to our promise. So I, along with several members of my staff, am here because I was invited here. I am here because I have organizational ties here.

But more basically, I am in Birmingham because injustice is

---

* AUTHOR'S NOTE: This response to a published statement by eight fellow clergymen from Alabama (Bishop C. C. J. Carpenter, Bishop Joseph A. Durick, Rabbi Hilton L. Grafman, Bishop Paul Hardin, Bishop Holan B. Harmon, the Reverend George M. Murray, the Reverend Edward V. Ramage and the Reverend Earl Stallings) was com-

here. Just as the prophets of the eighth century B.C. left their
villages and carried their "thus saith the Lord" far beyond the
boundaries of their home towns, and just as the Apostle Paul
left his village of Tarsus and carried the gospel of Jesus Christ
to the far corners of the Greco-Roman world, so am I compelled to carry the gospel of freedom beyond my own home
town. Like Paul, I must constantly respond to the Macedonian
call for aid.

Moreover, I am cognizant of the interrelatedness of all communities and states. I cannot sit idly by in Atlanta and not be
concerned about what happens in Birmingham. Injustice anywhere is a threat to justice everywhere. We are caught in an
inescapable network of mutuality, tied in a single garment of
destiny. Whatever affects one directly, affects all indirectly.
Never again can we afford to live with the narrow, provincial
"outside agitator" idea. Anyone who lives inside the United
States can never be considered an outsider anywhere within
its bounds.

You deplore the demonstrations taking place in Birmingham.
But your statement, I am sorry to say, fails to express a similar
concern for the conditions that brought about the demonstrations. I am sure that none of you would want to rest content
with the superficial kind of social analysis that deals merely
with effects and does not grapple with underlying causes. It is
unfortunate that demonstrations are taking place in Birmingham, but it is even more unfortunate that the city's white power
structure left the Negro community with no alternative.

In any nonviolent campaign there are four basic steps: collec-
tion of the facts to determine whether injustices exist; negotiation; self-purification; and direct action. We have gone through
all these steps in Birmingham. There can be no gainsaying the

posed under somewhat constricting circumstances. Begun on the margins
of the newspaper in which the statement appeared while I was in jail,
the letter was continued on scraps of writing paper supplied by a friendly
Negro trusty, and concluded on a pad my attorneys were eventually permitted to leave me. Although the text remains in substance unaltered, I
have indulged in the author's prerogative of polishing it for publication.

fact that racial injustice engulfs this community. Birmingham is probably the most thoroughly segregated city in the United States. Its ugly record of brutality is widely known. Negroes have experienced grossly unjust treatment in the courts. There have been more unsolved bombings of Negro homes and churches in Birmingham than in any other city in the nation. These are the hard, brutal facts of the case. On the basis of these conditions, Negro leaders sought to negotiate with the city fathers. But the latter consistently refused to engage in good-faith negotiation.

Then, last September, came the opportunity to talk with leaders of Birmingham's economic community. In the course of the negotiations, certain promises were made by the merchants—for example, to remove the stores' humiliating racial signs. On the basis of these promises, the Reverend Fred Shuttlesworth and the leaders of the Alabama Christian Movement for Human Rights agreed to a moratorium on all demonstrations. As the weeks and months went by, we realized that we were the victims of a broken promise. A few signs, briefly removed, returned; the others remained.

As in so many past experiences, our hopes had been blasted, and the shadow of deep disappointment settled upon us. We had no alternative except to prepare for direct action, whereby we would present our very bodies as a means of laying our case before the conscience of the local and the national community. Mindful of the difficulties involved, we decided to undertake a process of self-purification. We began a series of workshops on nonviolence, and we repeatedly asked ourselves: "Are you able to accept blows without retaliating?" "Are you able to endure the ordeal of jail?" We decided to schedule our direct-action program for the Easter season, realizing that except for Christmas, this is the main shopping period of the year. Knowing that a strong economic-withdrawal program would be the by-product of direct action, we felt that this would be the best time to bring pressure to bear on the merchants for the needed change.

Then it occurred to us that Birmingham's mayoral election

was coming up in March, and we speedily decided to postpone action until after election day. When we discovered that the Commissioner of Public Safety, Eugene "Bull" Connor, had piled up enough votes to be in the run-off, we decided again to postpone action until the day after the run-off so that the demonstrations could not be used to cloud the issues. Like many others, we waited to see Mr. Connor defeated, and to this end we endured postponement. Having aided in this community need, we felt that our direct-action program could be delayed no longer.

You may well ask: "Why direct action? Why sit-ins, marches and so forth? Isn't negotiation a better path?" You are quite right in calling for negotiation. Indeed, this is the very purpose of direct action. Nonviolent direct action seeks to create such a crisis and foster such a tension that a community which has constantly refused to negotiate is forced to confront the issue. It seeks so to dramatize the issue that it can no longer be ignored. My citing the creation of tension as part of the work of the nonviolent-resister may sound rather shocking. But I must confess that I am not afraid of the word "tension." I have earnestly opposed violent tension, but there is a type of constructive, nonviolent tension which is necessary for growth. Just as Socrates felt that it was necessary to create a tension in the mind so that individuals could rise from the bondage of myths and half-truths to the unfettered realm of creative analysis and objective appraisal, so must we see the need for nonviolent gadflies to create the kind of tension in society that will help men rise from the dark depths of prejudice and racism to the majestic heights of understanding and brotherhood.

The purpose of our direct-action program is to create a situation so crisis-packed that it will inevitably open the door to negotiation. I therefore concur with you in your call for negotiation. Too long has our beloved Southland been bogged down in a tragic effort to live in monologue rather than dialogue.

One of the basic points in your statement is that the action that I and my associates have taken in Birmingham is untimely.

Some have asked: "Why didn't you give the new city administration time to act?" The only answer that I can give to this query is that the new Birmingham administration must be prodded about as much as the out-going one, before it will act. We are sadly mistaken if we feel that the election of Albert Boutwell as mayor will bring the millennium to Birmingham. While Mr. Boutwell is a much more gentle person than Mr. Connor, they are both segregationists, dedicated to maintenance of the status quo. I have hope that Mr. Boutwell will be reasonable enough to see the futility of massive resistance to desegregation. But he will not see this without pressure from devotees of civil rights. My friends, I must say to you that we have not made a single gain in civil rights without determined legal and nonviolent pressure. Lamentably, it is an historical fact that privileged groups seldom give up their privileges voluntarily. Individuals may see the moral light and voluntarily give up their unjust posture; but, as Reinhold Niebuhr has reminded us, groups tend to be more immoral than individuals.

We know through painful experience that freedom is never voluntarily given by the oppressor; it must be demanded by the oppressed. Frankly, I have yet to engage in a direct-action campaign that was "well timed" in the view of those who have not suffered unduly from the disease of segregation. For years now I have heard the word "Wait!" It rings in the ear of every Negro with piercing familiarity. This "Wait" has almost always meant "Never." We must come to see, with one of our distinguished jurists, that "justice too long delayed is justice denied."

We have waited for more than 340 years for our constitutional and God-given rights. The nations of Asia and Africa are moving with jetlike speed toward gaining political independence, but we still creep at horse-and-buggy pace toward gaining a cup of coffee at a lunch counter. Perhaps it is easy for those who have never felt the stinging darts of segregation to say, "Wait." But when you have seen vicious mobs lynch your mothers and fathers at will and drown your sisters and brothers at whim; when you have seen hate-filled policemen curse, kick and even kill your black brothers and sisters; when you see the vast majority of your twenty million Negro brothers smothering in an airtight cage of poverty in the midst of an affluent society; when you suddenly find your tongue twisted and your speech stammering as you seek to explain to your six-year-old daughter why she can't go to the public amusement park that has just been advertised on television, and see tears welling up in her eyes when she is told that Funtown is closed to colored children, and see ominous clouds of inferiority beginning to form in her little mental sky, and see her beginning to distort her personality by developing an unconscious bitterness toward white people; when you have to concoct an answer for a five-year-old son who is asking: "Daddy, why do white people treat colored people so mean?"; when you take a cross-country drive and find it necessary to sleep night after night in the uncomfortable corners of your automobile because no motel will accept you; when you are humiliated day in and day out by nagging signs reading "white" and "colored"; when your first name becomes "nigger," your middle name becomes "boy" (however old you are) and your last name becomes "John," and your wife and mother are never given the respected title "Mrs."; when you are harried by day and haunted by night by the fact that you are a Negro, living constantly at tiptoe stance, never quite knowing what to expect next, and are plagued with inner fears and outer resentments; when you are forever fighting a degenerating sense of "nobodiness"—then you will understand why we find it difficult to wait. There comes a time when the cup of endurance runs over, and men are no longer willing to be plunged into the abyss of despair. I hope, sirs, you can understand our legitimate and unavoidable impatience.

You express a great deal of anxiety over our willingness to break laws. This is certainly a legitimate concern. Since we so diligently urge people to obey the Supreme Court's decision of 1954 outlawing segregation in the public schools, at first glance it may seem rather paradoxical for us consciously to break laws. One may well ask: "How can you advocate breaking some laws and obeying others?" The answer lies in the fact that there are two types of laws: just and unjust. I would be the first to advocate obeying just laws. One has not only a legal but a moral responsibility to obey just laws. Conversely, one has a moral responsibility to disobey unjust laws. I would agree with St. Augustine that "an unjust law is no law at all."

Now, what is the difference between the two? How does one determine whether a law is just or unjust? A just law is a man-made code that squares with the moral law or the law of God. An unjust law is a code that is out of harmony with the moral law. To put it in the terms of St. Thomas Aquinas: An unjust law is a human law that is not rooted in eternal law and natural law. Any law that uplifts human personality is just. Any law that degrades human personality is unjust. All segregation statutes are unjust because segregation distorts the soul and damages the personality. It gives the segregator a false sense of superiority and the segregated a false sense of inferiority. Segregation, to use the terminology of the Jewish philosopher Martin Buber, substitutes an "I-it" relationship for an "I-thou" relationship and ends up relegating persons to the status of things. Hence segregation is not only politically, economically and sociologically unsound, it is morally wrong and sinful. Paul Tillich has said that sin is separation. Is not segregation an existential expression of man's tragic separation, his awful estrangement, his terrible sinfulness? Thus it is that I can urge men to obey the 1954 decision of the Supreme Court, for it is morally right; and I can urge them to disobey segregation ordinances, for they are morally wrong.

Let us consider a more concrete example of just and unjust laws. An unjust law is a code that a numerical or power majority group compels a minority group to obey but does not make binding on itself. This is *difference* made legal. By the same token, a just law is a code that a majority compels a minority to follow and that it is willing to follow itself. This is *sameness* made legal.

Let me give another explanation. A law is unjust if it is

inflicted on a minority that, as a result of being denied the right to vote, had no part in enacting or devising the law. Who can say that the legislature of Alabama which set up that state's segregation laws was democratically elected? Throughout Alabama all sorts of devious methods are used to prevent Negroes from becoming registered voters, and there are some counties in which, even though Negroes constitute a majority of the population, not a single Negro is registered. Can any law enacted under such circumstances be considered democratically structured?

Sometimes a law is just on its face and unjust in its application. For instance, I have been arrested on a charge of parading without a permit. Now, there is nothing wrong in having an ordinance which requires a permit for a parade. But such an ordinance becomes unjust when it is used to maintain segregation and to deny citizens the First-Amendment privilege of peaceful assembly and protest.

I hope you are able to see the distinction I am trying to point out. In no sense do I advocate evading or defying the law, as would the rabid segregationist. That would lead to anarchy. One who breaks an unjust law must do so openly, lovingly, and with a willingness to accept the penalty. I submit that an individual who breaks a law that conscience tells him is unjust, and who willingly accepts the penalty of imprisonment in order to arouse the conscience of the community over its injustice, is in reality expressing the highest respect for law.

Of course, there is nothing new about this kind of civil disobedience. It was evidenced sublimely in the refusal of Shadrach, Meshach and Abednego to obey the laws of Nebuchadnezzar, on the ground that a higher moral law was at stake. It was practiced superbly by the early Christians, who were willing to face hungry lions and the excruciating pain of chopping blocks rather than submit to certain unjust laws of the Roman Empire. To a degree, academic freedom is a reality today because Socrates practiced civil disobedience. In our own nation, the Boston Tea Party represented a massive act of civil disobedience.

We should never forget that everything Adolf Hitler did in Germany was "legal" and everything the Hungarian freedom fighters did in Hungary was "illegal." It was "illegal" to aid and comfort a Jew in Hitler's Germany. Even so, I am sure that, had I lived in Germany at the time, I would have aided and comforted my Jewish brothers. If today I lived in a Communist country where certain principles dear to the Christian faith are suppressed, I would openly advocate disobeying that country's antireligious laws.

I must make two honest confessions to you, my Christian and Jewish brothers. First, I must confess that over the past few years I have been gravely disappointed with the white moderate. I have almost reached the regrettable conclusion that the Negro's great stumbling block in his stride toward freedom is not the White Citizen's Counciler or the Ku Klux Klanner, but the white moderate, who is more devoted to "order" than to justice; who prefers a negative peace which is the absence of tension to a positive peace which is the presence of justice; who constantly says: "I agree with you in the goal you seek, but I cannot agree with your methods of direct action"; who paternalistically believes he can set the timetable for another man's freedom; who lives by a mythical concept of time and who constantly advises the Negro to wait for a "more convenient season." Shallow understanding from people of good will is more frustrating than absolute misunderstanding from people of ill will. Lukewarm acceptance is much more bewildering than outright rejection.

I had hoped that the white moderate would understand that law and order exist for the purpose of establishing justice and that when they fail in this purpose they become the dangerously structured dams that block the flow of social progress. I had hoped that the white moderate would understand that the present tension in the South is a necessary phase of the transition from an obnoxious negative peace, in which the Negro passively accepted his unjust plight, to a substantive and positive peace, in which all men will respect the dignity and worth of human personality. Actually, we who engage in nonviolent

direct action are not the creators of tension. We merely bring
to the surface the hidden tension that is already alive. We bring
it out in the open, where it can be seen and dealt with. Like a
boil that can never be cured so long as it is covered up but
must be opened with all its ugliness to the natural medicines
of air and light, injustice must be exposed, with all the tension
its exposure creates, to the light of human conscience and the
air of national opinion before it can be cured.

In your statement you assert that our actions, even though
peaceful, must be condemned because they precipitate violence.
But is this a logical assertion? Isn't this like condemning a
robbed man because his possession of money precipitated the
evil act of robbery? Isn't this like condemning Socrates because
his unswerving commitment to truth and his philosophical in-
quiries precipitated the act by the misguided populace in which
they made him drink hemlock? Isn't this like condemning
Jesus because his unique God-consciousness and never-ceasing
devotion to God's will precipitated the evil act of crucifixion?
We must come to see that, as the federal courts have consistently affirmed, it is wrong to urge an individual to cease his
efforts to gain his basic constitutional rights because the quest
may precipitate violence. Society must protect the robbed and
punish the robber.

I had also hoped that the white moderate would reject the
myth concerning time in relation to the struggle for freedom.
I have just received a letter from a white brother in Texas.
He writes: "All Christians know that the colored people will
receive equal rights eventually, but it is possible that you are
in too great a religious hurry. It has taken Christianity almost
two thousand years to accomplish what it has. The teachings
of Christ take time to come to earth." Such an attitude stems
from a tragic misconception of time, from the strangely irra-
tional notion that there is something in the very flow of time
that will inevitably cure all ills. Actually, time itself is neutral;
it can be used either destructively or constructively. More and
more I feel that the people of ill will have used time much

more effectively than have the people of good will. We will have to repent in this generation not merely for the hateful words and actions of the bad people but for the appalling silence of the good people. Human progress never rolls in on wheels of inevitability; it comes through the tireless efforts of men willing to be co-workers with God, and without this hard work, time itself becomes an ally of the forces of social stagnation. We must use time creatively, in the knowledge that the time is always ripe to do right. Now is the time to make real the promise of democracy and transform our pending national elegy into a creative psalm of brotherhood. Now is the time to lift our national policy from the quicksand of racial injustice to the solid rock of human dignity.

You speak of our activity in Birmingham as extreme. At first I was rather disappointed that fellow clergymen would see my nonviolent efforts as those of an extremist. I began thinking about the fact that I stand in the middle of two opposing forces in the Negro community. One is a force of complacency, made up in part of Negroes who, as a result of long years of oppression, are so drained of self-respect and a sense of "somebodiness" that they have adjusted to segregation; and in part of a few middle-class Negroes who, because of a degree of academic and economic security and because in some ways they profit by segregation, have become insensitive to the problems of the masses. The other force is one of bitterness and hatred, and it comes perilously close to advocating violence. It is expressed in the various black nationalist groups that are springing up across the nation, the largest and best-known being Elijah Muhammad's Muslim movement. Nourished by the Negro's frustration over the continued existence of racial discrimination, this movement is made up of people who have lost faith in America, who have absolutely repudiated Christianity, and who have concluded that the white man is an incorrigible "devil."

I have tried to stand between these two forces, saying that we need emulate neither the "do-nothingism" of the complacent nor the hatred and despair of the black nationalist. For there is the more excellent way of love and nonviolent protest. I am grateful to God that, through the influence of the Negro church, the way of nonviolence became an integral part of our struggle.

If this philosophy had not emerged, by now many streets of the South would, I am convinced, be flowing with blood. And I am further convinced that if our white brothers dismiss as "rabble-rousers" and "outside agitators" those of us who employ nonviolent direct action, and if they refuse to support our nonviolent efforts, millions of Negroes will, out of frustration and despair, seek solace and security in black-nationalist ideologies—a development that would inevitably lead to a frightening racial nightmare.

Oppressed people cannot remain oppressed forever. The yearning for freedom eventually manifests itself, and that is what has happend to the American Negro. Something within has reminded him of his birthright of freedom, and something without has reminded him that it can be gained. Consciously or unconsciously, he has been caught up by the *Zeitgeist*, and with his black brothers of Africa and his brown and yellow brothers of Asia, South America and the Caribbean, the United States Negro is moving with a sense of great urgency toward the promised land of racial justice. If one recognizes this vital urge that has engulfed the Negro community, one should readily understand why public demonstrations are taking place. The Negro has many pent-up resentments and latent frustrations, and he must release them. So let him march; let him make prayer pilgrimages to the city hall; let him go on freedom rides—and try to understand why he must do so. If his repressed emotions are not released in nonviolent ways, they will seek expression through violence; this is not a threat but a fact of history. So I have not said to my people: "Get rid of your discontent." Rather, I have tried to say that this normal and healthy discontent can be channeled into the creative outlet of nonviolent direct action. And now this approach is being termed extremist.

But though I was initially disappointed at being categorized as an extremist, as I continued to think about the matter I gradually gained a measure of satisfaction from the label. Was not Jesus an extremist for love: "Love your enemies, bless them that curse you, do good to them that hate you, and pray for them which despitefully use you, and persecute you." Was not Amos an extremist for justice: "Let justice roll down like waters and righteousness like an ever-flowing stream." Was not Paul an extremist for the Christian gospel: "I bear in my body the marks of the Lord Jesus." Was not Martin Luther an extremist: "Here I stand; I cannot do otherwise, so help me God." And John Bunyan: "I will stay in jail to the end of my days before I make a butchery of my conscience." And Abraham Lincoln: "This nation cannot survive half slave and half free." And Thomas Jefferson: "We hold these truths to be self-evident, that all men are created equal . . ." So the question is not whether we will be extremists, but what kind of extremists we will be. Will we be extremists for hate or for love? Will we be extremists for the preservation of justice or for the extension of justice? In that dramatic scene on Calvary's hill three men were crucified. We must never forget that all three were crucified for the same crime—the crime of extremism. Two were extremists for immorality, and thus fell below their environment. The other, Jesus Christ, was an extremist for love, truth and goodness, and thereby rose above his environment. Perhaps the South, the nation and the world are in dire need of creative extremists.

I had hoped that the white moderate would see this need. Perhaps I was too optimistic; perhaps I expected too much. I suppose I should have realized that few members of the oppressor race can understand the deep groans and passionate yearnings of the oppressed race, and still fewer have the vision to see that injustice must be rooted out by strong, persistent and determined action. I am thankful, however, that some of our white brothers in the South have grasped the meaning of this social revolution and committed themselves to it. They are still all too few in quantity, but they are big in quality. Some—

such as Ralph McGill, Lillian Smith, Harry Golden, James McBride Dabbs, Ann Braden and Sarah Patton Boyle—have written about our struggle in eloquent and prophetic terms. Others have marched with us down nameless streets of the South. They have languished in filthy, roach-infested jails, suffering the abuse and brutality of policemen who view them as "dirty nigger-lovers." Unlike so many of their moderate brothers and sisters, they have recognized the urgency of the moment and sensed the need for powerful "action" antidotes to combat the disease of segregation.

Let me take note of my other major disappointment. I have been so greatly disappointed with the white church and its leadership. Of course, there are some notable exceptions. I am not unmindful of the fact that each of you has taken some significant stands on this issue. I commend you, Reverend Stallings, for your Christian stand on this past Sunday, in welcoming Negroes to your worship service on a nonsegregated basis. I commend the Catholic leaders of this state for integrating Spring Hill College several years ago.

But despite these notable exceptions, I must honestly reiterate that I have been disappointed with the church. I do not say this as one of those negative critics who can always find something wrong with the church. I say this as a minister of the gospel, who loves the church; who was nurtured in its bosom; who has been sustained by its spiritual blessings and who will remain true to it as long as the cord of life shall lengthen.

When I was suddenly catapulted into the leadership of the bus protest in Montgomery, Alabama, a few years ago, I felt we would be supported by the white church. I felt that the white ministers, priests and rabbis of the South would be among our strongest allies. Instead, some have been outright opponents, refusing to understand the freedom movement and misrepresenting its leaders; all too many others have been more cautious than courageous and have remained silent behind the anesthetizing security of stained-glass windows.

In spite of my shattered dreams, I came to Birmingham with

the hope that the white religious leadership of this community would see the justice of our cause and, with deep moral concern, would serve as the channel through which our just grievances could reach the power structure. I had hoped that each of you would understand. But again I have been disappointed.

I have heard numerous southern religious leaders admonish their worshipers to comply with a desegregation decision because it is the law, but I have longed to hear white ministers declare: "Follow this decree because integration is morally right and because the Negro is your brother." In the midst of blatant injustices inflicted upon the Negro, I have watched white churchmen stand on the sideline and mouth pious irrelevancies and sanctimonious trivialities. In the midst of a mighty struggle to rid our nation of racial and economic injustice, I have heard many ministers say: "Those are social issues, with which the gospel has no real concern." And I have watched many churches commit themselves to a completely otherworldly religion which makes a strange, un-Biblical distinction between body and soul, between the sacred and the secular.

I have traveled the length and breadth of Alabama, Mississippi and all the other southern states. On sweltering summer days and crisp autumn mornings I have looked at the South's beautiful churches with their lofty spires pointing heavenward. I have beheld the impressive outlines of her massive religious-education buildings. Over and over I have found myself asking: "What kind of people worship here? Who is their God? Where were their voices when the lips of Governor Barnett dripped with words of interposition and nullification? Where were they when Governor Wallace gave a clarion call for defiance and hatred? Where were their voices of support when bruised and weary Negro men and women decided to rise from the dark dungeons of complacency to the bright hills of creative protest?"

Yes, these questions are still in my mind. In deep disappointment I have wept over the laxity of the church. But be assured that my tears have been tears of love. There can be no deep disappointment where there is not deep love. Yes, I love the church. How could I do otherwise? I am in the rather unique position of being the son, the grandson and the great-grandson of preachers. Yes, I see the church as the body of Christ. But, oh! How we have blemished and scarred that body through social neglect and through fear of being nonconformists.

There was a time when the church was very powerful—in the time when the early Christians rejoiced at being deemed worthy to suffer for what they believed. In those days the church was not merely a thermometer that recorded the ideas and principles of popular opinion; it was a thermostat that transformed the mores of society. Whenever the early Christians entered a town, the people in power became disturbed and immediately sought to convict the Christians for being "disturbers of the peace" and "outside agitators." But the Christians pressed on, in the conviction that they were "a colony of heaven," called to obey God rather than man. Small in number, they were big in commitment. They were too God-intoxicated to be "astronomically intimidated." By their effort and example they brought an end to such ancient evils as infanticide and gladiatorial contests.

Things are different now. So often the contemporary church is a weak, ineffectual voice with an uncertain sound. So often it is an archdefender of the status quo. Far from being disturbed by the presence of the church, the power structure of the average community is consoled by the church's silent—and often even vocal—sanction of things as they are.

But the judgment of God is upon the church as never before. If today's church does not recapture the sacrificial spirit of the early church, it will lose its authenticity, forfeit the loyalty of millions, and be dismissed as an irrelevant social club with no meaning for the twentieth century. Every day I meet young people whose disappointment with the church has turned into outright disgust.

Perhaps I have once again been too optimistic. Is organized religion too inextricably bound to the status quo to save our nation and the world? Perhaps I must turn my faith to the inner spiritual church, the church within the church, as the true *ekklesia* and the hope of the world. But again I am thankful to God that some noble souls from the ranks of organized religion have broken loose from the paralyzing chains of conformity and joined us as active partners in the struggle for freedom. They have left their secure congregations and walked the streets of Albany, Georgia, with us. They have gone down the highways of the South on tortuous rides for freedom. Yes, they have gone to jail with us. Some have been dismissed from their churches, have lost the support of their bishops and fellow ministers. But they have acted in the faith that right defeated is stronger than evil triumphant. Their witness has been the spiritual salt that has preserved the true meaning of the gospel in these troubled times. They have carved a tunnel of hope through the dark mountain of disappointment.

I hope the church as a whole will meet the challenge of this decisive hour. But even if the church does not come to the aid of justice, I have no despair about the future. I have no fear about the outcome of our struggle in Birmingham, even if our motives are at present misunderstood. We will reach the goal of freedom in Birmingham and all over the nation, because the goal of America is freedom. Abused and scorned though we may be, our destiny is tied up with America's destiny. Before the pilgrims landed at Plymouth, we were here. Before the pen of Jefferson etched the majestic words of the Declaration of Independence across the pages of history, we were here. For more than two centuries our forebears labored in this country without wages; they made cotton king; they built the homes of their masters while suffering gross injustice and shameful humiliation—and yet out of a bottomless vitality they continued to thrive and develop. If the inexpressible cruelties of slavery could not stop us, the opposition we now face will surely fail. We will win our freedom because the sacred heritage of our nation and the eternal will of God are embodied in our echoing demands.

Before closing I feel impelled to mention one other point in your statement that has troubled me profoundly. You warmly commended the Birmingham police force for keeping "order" and "preventing violence." I doubt that you would have so warmly commended the police force if you had seen its dogs sinking their teeth into unarmed, nonviolent Negroes. I doubt that you would so quickly commend the policemen if you were to observe their ugly and inhumane treatment of Negroes here in the city jail; if you were to watch them push and curse old Negro women and young Negro girls; if you were to see them slap and kick old Negro men and young boys; if you were to observe them, as they did on two occasions, refuse to give us food because we wanted to sing our grace together. I cannot join you in your praise of the Birmingham police department.

It is true that the police have exercised a degree of discipline in handling the demonstrators. In this sense they have conducted themselves rather "nonviolently" in public. But for what purpose? To preserve the evil system of segregation. Over the past few years I have consistently preached that nonviolence demands that the means we use must be as pure as the ends we seek. I have tried to make clear that it is wrong to use immoral means to attain moral ends. But now I must affirm that it is just as wrong, or perhaps even more so, to use moral means to preserve immoral ends. Perhaps Mr. Connor and his policemen have been rather nonviolent in public, as was Chief Pritchett in Albany, Georgia, but they have used the moral means of nonviolence to maintain the immoral end of racial injustice. As T. S. Eliot has said: "The last temptation is the greatest treason: To do the right deed for the wrong reason."

I wish you had commended the Negro sit-inners and demonstrators of Birmingham for their sublime courage, their willingness to suffer and their amazing discipline in the midst of great provocation. One day the South will recognize its real heroes. They will be the James Merediths, with the noble sense of purpose that enables them to face jeering and hostile mobs, and with the agonizing loneliness that characterizes the life of the pioneer. They will be old, oppressed, battered Negro women, symbolized in a seventy-two-year-old woman in Montgomery, Alabama, who rose up with a sense of dignity and with her people decided not to ride segregated buses, and who responded with ungrammatical profundity to one who inquired about her weariness: "My feets is tired, but my soul is at rest." They will be the young high school and college students, the young ministers of the gospel and a host of their elders, courageously and nonviolently sitting in at lunch counters and willingly going to jail for conscience' sake. One day the South will know that when these disinherited children of God sat down at lunch counters, they were in reality standing up for what is best in the American dream and for the most sacred values in our Judaeo-Christian heritage, thereby bringing our nation back to those great wells of democracy which were dug deep by the founding fathers in their formulation of the Constitution and the Declaration of Independence.

Never before have I written so long a letter. I'm afraid it is much too long to take your precious time. I can assure you that it would have been much shorter if I had been writing from a comfortable desk, but what else can one do when he is alone in a narrow jail cell, other than write long letters, think long thoughts and pray long prayers?

If I have said anything in this letter that overstates the truth and indicates an unreasonable impatience, I beg you to forgive me. If I have said anything that understates the truth and indicates my having a patience that allows me to settle for anything less than brotherhood, I beg God to forgive me.

I hope this letter finds you strong in the faith. I also hope that circumstances will soon make it possible for me to meet each of you, not as an integrationist or a civil-rights leader but as a fellow clergyman and a Christian brother. Let us all hope that the dark clouds of racial prejudice will soon pass away and the deep fog of misunderstanding will be lifted from our fear-drenched communities, and in some not too distant tomorrow the radiant stars of love and brotherhood will shine over our great nation with all their scintillating beauty.

Yours for the cause of Peace and Brotherhood,

MARTIN LUTHER KING, JR.

10. . . . A Moral Issue

John F. Kennedy Appeals to the Nation—1963

On June 10, 1963, Governor George C. Wallace arrived in Tuscaloosa to oppose the court-ordered admission of two Negroes to the University of Alabama. On June 11, President John F. Kennedy issued a proclamation on unlawful obstructions of justice in Alabama and an Executive Order authorizing the use of the armed forces there.

The President's proclamation, signed by him and Dean Rusk, Secretary of State, criticized "the Governor and forces under his command" for proposed action opposing "the execution of the laws of the United States" and threats "to impede the course of justice under those laws."

The year before, in his State of the Union message, President Kennedy had called upon the Federal Government and the nation to "get on" with civil rights, in which there was "much still to be done—by the Executive, by the courts, and by Congress." In another message, he had lauded the efforts of civil rights champions for "spurring the nation on to the essential goal of securing the full constitutional rights of our citizens." Now, on June 11, 1963, he used the Alabama incident to announce the Administration's civil rights proposals asking Congress "to make a commitment it has not fully made in this century."

More than that, he added a new dimension to the struggle itself. "This is not . . . a legal or legislative issue alone . . . We are confronted primarily with a moral issue," the President declared.

The following week, Mr. Kennedy sent his civil rights proposals to Congress—"necessary measures which only the Congress can provide, and they must be provided at this session."

Two months later—August 29—thousands of Americans, white and Negro, representing all faiths and all walks of life, converged on Washington to urge, by their presence, passage of a civil rights law. These were the leaders: Matthew Ahmann, executive director of the National Catholic Conference for Interracial Justice; Dr. Eugene Carson Blake, chief executive officer of the United Presbyterian Church in the U.S.A.; Martin Luther King, Jr., president of the Southern Christian Leadership Conference; John Lewis, chairman of the Student Non-Violent Coordinating Committee; Floyd B. McKissick, national chairman of the Congress of Racial Equality, marching for President James Farmer who was in a Louisiana jail; Rabbi Joachim Prinz, president of the American Jewish Congress; Walter P. Reuther, president of the United Automobile Workers Union; Roy Wilkins, executive secretary of the National Association for the Advancement of Colored People; Whitney M. Young, Jr., executive director of the National Urban League—and as the director of the March On Washington, A. Philip Randolph, organizer of the 1941 March movement which had prompted President Roosevelt to establish the wartime Fair Employment Practices Commission.

"We are gathered here in the largest demonstration in the history of this nation," Randolph said. "Let the nation and the world know the meaning of our numbers. . . . We are the advance guard of a moral revolution."

The struggle had taken on added intensity and new allies— no-longer-complacent white Americans, committed as never before to what President Kennedy called the nation's "moral crisis."

AN ADDRESS BY JOHN F. KENNEDY
JUNE 11, 1963

My fellow citizens.

This afternoon, following a series of threats and defiant statements, the presence of Alabama National Guardsmen was required on the University of Alabama to carry out the final and unequivocal order of the United States District Court of the Northern District of Alabama.

That order called for the admission of two clearly qualified young Alabama residents who happened to have been born Negro.

That they were admitted peacefully on the campus is due in good measure to the conduct of the students of the University of Alabama who met their responsibilities in a constructive way.

I hope that every American, regardless of where he lives, will stop and examine his conscience about this and other related incidents.

This nation was founded by men of many nations and backgrounds. It was founded on the principle that all men are created equal, and that the rights of every man are diminished when the rights of one man are threatened.

Today we are committed to a worldwide struggle to promote and protect the rights of all who wish to be free. And when Americans are sent to Vietnam or West Berlin we do not ask for whites only.

It ought to be possible, therefore, for American students of any color to attend any public institution they select without having to be backed up by troops. It ought to be possible for American consumers of any color to receive equal service in places of public accommodation, such as hotels and restaurants, and theaters and retail stores without being forced to resort to demonstrations in the street.

And it ought to be possible for American citizens of any

color to register and to vote in a free election without interference or fear of reprisal.

It ought to be possible, in short, for every American to enjoy the privileges of being American without regard to his race or his color.

In short, every American ought to have the right to be treated as he would wish to be treated, as one would wish his children to be treated. But this is not the case.

The Negro baby born in America today, regardless of the section or the state in which he is born, has about one-half as much chance of completing high school as a white baby, born in the same place, on the same day; one-third as much chance of completing college; one-third as much chance of becoming a professional man; twice as much chance of becoming unemployed; about one-seventh as much chance of earning $10,000 a year; a life expectancy which is seven years shorter and the prospects of earning only half as much.

This is not a sectional issue. Difficulties over segregation and discrimination exist in every city, in every state of the Union, producing in many cities a rising tide of discontent that threatens the public safety.

Nor is this a partisan issue. In a time of domestic crisis, men of goodwill and generosity should be able to unite regardless of party or politics.

This is not even a legal or legislative issue alone. It is better to settle these matters in the courts than on the streets, and new laws are needed at every level. But law alone cannot make men see right.

We are confronted primarily with a moral issue. It is as old as the Scriptures and is as clear as the American Constitution. The heart of the question is whether all Americans are to be afforded equal rights and equal opportunities; whether we are going to treat our fellow Americans as we want to be treated.

If an American, because his skin is dark, cannot eat lunch in a restaurant open to the public; if he cannot send his children to the best public school available; if he cannot vote for the public officials who represent him; if, in short, he cannot enjoy the full and free life which all of us want, then who among us would be content to have the color of his skin changed and stand in his place?

Who among us would then be content with the counsels of patience and delay? One hundred years of delay have passed since President Lincoln freed the slaves, yet their heirs, their grandsons, are not fully free. They are not yet freed from the bonds of injustice; they are not yet freed from social and economic oppression.

And this nation, for all its hopes and all its boasts, will not be fully free until all its citizens are free.

We preach freedom around the world, and we mean it. And we cherish our freedom here at home. But are we to say to the world—and much more importantly to each other—that this is the land of the free, except for the Negroes; that we have no second-class citizens, except Negroes; that we have no class or caste system, no ghettos, no master race, except with respect to Negroes?

Now the time has come for this nation to fulfill its promise. The events in Birmingham and elsewhere have so increased the cries for equality that no city or state or legislative body can prudently choose to ignore them.

The fires of frustration and discord are burning in every city, North and South. Where legal remedies are not at hand, redress is sought in the streets in demonstrations, parades and protests, which create tensions and threaten violence—and threaten lives.

We face, therefore, a moral crisis as a country and a people. It cannot be met by repressive police action. It cannot be left to increased demonstrations in the streets. It cannot be quieted by token moves or talk. It is a time to act in the Congress, in your state and local legislative body, and, above all, in all of our daily lives.

It is not enough to pin the blame on others, to say this is a problem of one section of the country or another, or deplore the facts that we face. A great change is at hand, and our task, our obligation, is to make that revolution, that change, peaceful and constructive for all.

Those who do nothing are inviting shame as well as violence. Those who act boldly are recognizing right as well as reality.

Next week I shall ask the Congress of the United States to act, to make a commitment it has not fully made in this century to the proposition that race has no place in American life or law.

The Federal judiciary has upheld that proposition in a series of forthright cases. The Executive Branch has adopted that proposition in the conduct of its affairs, including the employment of Federal personnel, and the use of Federal facilities, and the sale of Federally financed housing.

But there are other necessary measures which only the Congress can provide, and they must be provided at this session.

The old code of equity law under which we live commands for every wrong a remedy. But in too many communities, in too many parts of the country, wrongs are inflicted on Negro citizens and there are no remedies in law. Unless the Congress acts, their only remedy is the street.

I am, therefore, asking the Congress to enact legislation giving all Americans the right to be served in facilities which are open to the public—hotels, restaurants and theaters, retail stores and similar establishments. This seems to me to be an elementary right. Its denial is an arbitrary indignity that no American in 1963 should have to endure, but many do.

I have recently met with scores of business leaders, urging them to take voluntary action to end this discrimination. And I have been encouraged by their response. And in the last two weeks, over seventy-five cities have seen progress made in de-segregating these kinds of facilities.

But many are unwilling to act alone. And for this reason nationwide legislation is needed, if we are to move this problem from the streets to the courts.

I am also asking Congress to authorize the Federal Government to participate more fully in lawsuits designed to end segregation in public education. We have succeeded in persuading many districts to desegregate voluntarily. Dozens have admitted Negroes without violence.

Today a Negro is attending a state-supported institution in every one of our fifty states. But the pace is very slow.

Too many Negro children entering segregated grade schools at the time of the Supreme Court's decision nine years ago will enter segregated high schools this fall, having suffered a loss which can never be restored.

The lack of an adequate education denies the Negro a chance to get a decent job. The orderly implementation of the Supreme Court decision, therefore, cannot be left solely to those who may not have the economic resources to carry their legal action or who may be subject to harassment. Other features will be also requested, including greater protection for the right to vote.

But legislation, I repeat, cannot solve this problem alone. It must be solved in the homes of every American in every community across our country.

In this respect, I want to pay tribute to those citizens, North and South, who have been working in their communities to make life better for all.

They are acting not out of a sense of legal duty but out of a sense of human decency. Like our soldiers and sailors in all parts of the world, they are meeting freedom's challenge on the firing line and I salute them for their honor—their courage.

My fellow Americans, this is a problem which faces us all, in every city of the North as well as the South.

Today there are Negroes unemployed—two or three times as many compared to whites; inadequate education; moving into the large cities, unable to find work; young people particularly out of work, without hope, denied equal rights, denied the opportunity to eat at a restaurant or a lunch counter, or go to a movie theater; denied the right to a decent education; denied almost, today, the right to attend a state university even though qualified.

It seems to me that these are matters which concern us all—

not merely Presidents, or Congressmen, or Governors, but every citizen of the United States.

This is one country. It has become one country because all of us and all the people who came here had an equal chance to develop their talents.

We cannot say to ten per cent of the population that "you can't have that right. Your children can't have the chance to develop whatever talents they have, that the only way that they are going to get their rights is to go in the street and demonstrate."

I think we owe them and we owe ourselves a better country than that.

Therefore, I am asking for your help in making it easier for us to move ahead and provide the kind of equality of treatment which we would want ourselves—to give a chance for every child to be educated to the limit of his talent.

As I have said before, not every child has an equal talent or an equal ability or equal motivation. But they should have the equal right to develop their talent and their ability and their motivation to make something of themselves.

We have a right to expect that the Negro community will be responsible, will uphold the law. But *they* have a right to expect the law will be fair, that the Constitution will be color-blind, as Justice Harlan said at the turn of the century.

This is what we are talking about. This is a matter which concerns this country and what it stands for, and in meeting it I ask the support of all of our citizens.

11. *An Idea Whose Time Has Come*

The Civil Rights Act of 1964

On June 19, 1964—just one year after President Kennedy had sent his civil rights proposal to Congress—the Senate passed the civil rights bill by the overwhelming vote of 73 to 27. Now it would go back to the House of Representatives for concurrence with the changes made since the House had passed the bill on February 10—by a vote of 290 to 130. With the support of the two men largely responsible for the House bill—Representative Emanuel Celler (D., N.Y.), and William M. McCullock (R., Ohio), acceptance of the Senate version was assured. On July 2, President Lyndon B. Johnson signed America's strongest civil rights bill into law.

> The purpose of this law is simple [President Johnson said]. It does not restrict the freedom of any American so long as he respects the rights of others. It does not give special treatment to any citizen. It does say the only limit to a man's hope for happiness and for the future of his children shall be his own ability. . . . Its purpose is to promote a more abiding commitment to freedom, a more constant pursuit of justice and a deeper respect for human dignity. . . . Let us lay aside irrelevant differences and make our nation whole.

The bill that was passed was not only essentially intact, but was broader and stronger than the draft sent to Congress by President Kennedy. It represented a year of words—the House filled 477 pages of the *Congressional Record* with civil rights debates lasting 73 hours 41 minutes over the 9 days from January 31 to February 10; the Senate filled 2,890 pages with 736 hours 10 minutes of debate.

Credited with getting the necessary votes for closure—to shut off filibuster—were Senators Everett N. Dirksen (R., Ill.) and Hubert H. Humphrey (D., Minn.). Together they gathered 71 votes, 4 more than needed. Dirksen, with no previous record of staunch support for civil rights, was praised for "saving the bill," for having pieced together a substitute for the House-passed bill so near to the original that it was acceptable to the Justice Department and the bipartisan civil rights coalition and sufficiently different in tone and emphasis to win the crucial Republican votes needed for closure.

Asked why he had worked so diligently, the Senator quoted Victor Hugo. On the night Hugo died, Dirksen declared, it is said that he wrote in his diary: "No army can withstand the strength of an idea whose time has come."

At last the legislative branch had caught up with the executive and judicial branches. An act of Congress had brought America's 20 million Negro citizens under the umbrella of the Constitution. The Civil Rights Act of 1964 would not automatically bring freedom but it would provide the firm legal foundation upon which freedom must stand. It would, if implemented, make equality the reality in American life that the Act made it in law.

No one expected implementation to be easy, but the climate for it was more favorable than ever before. Civil rights was indeed "an idea whose time has come."

A SUMMARY OF THE CIVIL RIGHTS ACT OF 1964 *

TITLE I: VOTING

The purpose of this section is to provide more effective enforcement of the right to vote in Federal elections (for President, Vice President, presidential electors or members of Congress) without regard to race or color. It also speeds up the procedure by which voting rights suits may be decided.

The Act:

a. requires that the same standards be applied to all individuals seeking to register and vote;

b. forbids denial of the right to vote because of some minor mistake or omission;

c. requires that only literacy tests that are written may be used as a qualification for voting; and that the tests and answers be available on request;

d. establishes that in voting rights law suits the court must presume that anyone who completed the sixth grade is literate, unless the State can prove otherwise.

In any voting suit brought by the Government charging that there is a "pattern or practice" of voting discrimination, either the Attorney General or the defendant may ask that a three-judge Federal court be appointed to hear the case. Appeals from the decisions of such a court may be taken directly to the Supreme Court.

TITLE II: PUBLIC ACCOMMODATIONS

Discrimination on the basis of race, color, religion or national origin is specifically forbidden in the following places of public accommodation:

a. hotels and motels, restaurants, lunch counters, movie houses, gasoline stations, theaters and stadiums;

* Prepared by the U. S. Commission on Civil Rights.

b. any other establishment which offers its services to patrons of the covered establishment; for example,

—a barbershop or tavern located in a hotel, or

—a department store in which there is a restaurant: *so long as* the covered facilities either affect interstate commerce in their operations, or are supported in their discriminatory practices by State action.

In addition, discrimination is forbidden in any other place of public accommodation that is required to segregate by State or local laws.

If there are no State or local laws requiring segregation, the Federal law does not cover:

a. barbershops, beauty parlors and other service establishments unless they are located in a hotel and offer these services to hotel guests;

b. retail stores that do not serve food, or places of recreation (except as listed above) which do not serve food;

c. lodging houses, hotels or similar places which take temporary guests if they have fewer than six rooms for rent in a building occupied by the owner.

Places that are actually owned and operated as private clubs are exempted from coverage of this title except to the extent that they offer their facilities to patrons of a covered establishment, such as a country club that customarily allows guests of a hotel to use its golf course.

No person may intimidate, threaten or coerce anyone for the purpose of interfering with the rights created by this title.

The provisions of this title may be enforced in two ways:

1. By *individual action* in a civil suit filed by the persons discriminated against, or

2. By *Government action* in a civil suit filed by the Attorney General.

In public accommodations suits filed by individuals:

—the court hearing the suit may appoint a lawyer for the person bringing the complaint and exempt the complainant from the payment of certain costs;

—the court may permit the Attorney General to enter the case;

—if there is a State law or local ordinance that prohibits discrimination, the complaint must first be taken to the State or local authorities, allowing them 30 days to begin a proceeding before suit can be filed in a Federal court;

—once the case is in court, the court can postpone action until the State or local proceeding is completed;

—if there are no State or local anti-discrimination provisions, the court may refer the matter to the Community Relations Service (see Title X) so that it may seek to secure voluntary compliance within no more than 120 days.

The Attorney General may file a public accommodations suit when he believes there is a pattern or practice of resistance. As in Title I voting suits, he may request a three-judge court for this action.

In public accommodations suits brought either by individuals or the Attorney General, the court may issue temporary or permanent injunctions or restraining orders against those found to be violating the law. A person or persons failing to obey such court decrees may be punished by contempt proceedings under the jury trials provision of the law (see Title XI).

TITLE III: PUBLIC FACILITIES

The Attorney General is authorized to bring a civil suit to compel desegregation of any publicly-owned or operated facility whenever he receives a written complaint of discrimination. He must believe that the complaint merits action and must certify that the individual or individuals making the complaint are themselves unable to take the necessary legal action. State or municipally owned or operated parks, libraries and hospitals are among the facilities covered.

Title IV: Public Education

Under this title the U. S. Office of Education is authorized to:

a. conduct a national survey to determine the availability of equal educational opportunity;

b. provide technical assistance, upon request, to help States, political subdivisions or school districts carry out school desegregation plans;

c. arrange training institutes to prepare teachers and other school personnel to deal with desegregation problems;

d. make grants enabling school boards to employ specialists for in-service training programs.

In addition, the Attorney General is authorized to file civil suits seeking to compel desegregation of public schools, including public colleges.

Before filing such a suit the Attorney General must have received a signed complaint from a pupil or parent and must have determined that the complainant, according to standards set forth in the Act, is unable to bring the action. The Attorney General is also required to notify the school board and give it a reasonable period of time to correct the alleged condition before filing suit.

Title V: Commission on Civil Rights

The life of the U. S. Commission on Civil Rights is extended until January 31, 1968. Since 1957 the Commission's functions have included investigating denials of the right to vote, studying legal developments and appraising Federal policies relating to equal protection of the laws, and making recommendations for corrective action to the President and the Congress.

Title V gives the Commission added authority to:

a. serve as a national clearinghouse for civil rights information;

b. investigate allegations of vote fraud.

Commission hearing procedures are amended to further protect the rights of individuals who may be affected by Commission proceedings.

As a national clearinghouse, the Commission will provide civil rights information in such areas as voting, housing, education, employment and the use of public facilities to Federal, State and local government agencies and officials, organizations and businesses, and the general public.

TITLE VI: FEDERALLY ASSISTED PROGRAMS

Under this title every Federal agency which provides financial assistance through grants, loans or contracts is required to eliminate discrimination on the grounds of race, color or national origin in these programs.

For example, this title would require the following:

a. hospitals constructed with Federal funds would have to serve all patients without regard to race, color or national origin;

b. elementary and secondary schools constructed, maintained and operated with Federal funds would have to admit children without regard to race, color or national origin;

c. State employment services financed by Federal funds would have to refer qualified job applicants for employment without discrimination;

d. schools for the deaf and the blind operated with Federal funds would have to serve the deaf and blind of any color;

e. colleges and universities receiving funds for their general operation or for the construction of special facilities, such as research centers, would have to admit students without discrimination;

f. construction contractors receiving funds under Federal public works programs would have to hire employees without discrimination.

Action by a Federal agency to carry out the requirements of

this title may include the terminating of programs where discrimination is taking place or refusal to grant assistance to such a program.

Each agency is required to publish rules or regulations to carry out the purposes of the title. These rules and regulations are subject to the approval of the President.

Compliance actions are subject to the following conditions:

a. notice must be given of alleged failure to comply and an opportunity for a hearing must be provided;

b. in the event assistance is to be cut off, a written report must be submitted to Congress 30 days before the cut-off date;

c. compliance action may be appealed to the courts.

Social security and veteran's benefits, and other Federal benefits distributed directly to individuals are not affected by this law.

Federal assistance in the form of insurance or guaranty—for example, FHA insured loans—are not covered by this title (however, the President's Executive Order prohibiting discrimination in Federally aided housing remains in effect).

Title VII: Equal Employment Opportunity

This title establishes a Federal right to equal opportunity in employment. It creates an Equal Employment Opportunity Commission to assist in implementing this right.

Employers, labor unions and employment agencies are required to treat all persons without regard to their race, color, religion, sex, or national origin. This treatment must be given in all phases of employment, including hiring, promotion, firing, apprenticeship and other training programs, and job assignments.

When this title goes into full effect employers will be subject to its provisions if they have 25 or more regular employees in an industry that affects interstate commerce. Generally speaking, labor unions will be subject to the Act if they either operate a hiring hall for covered employers, or if they have 25 or more members who are employed by a covered employer. Employment agencies are also included if they regularly undertake to supply employees for a covered employer.

(Enforcement of the nondiscrimination requirements for employers and unions is postponed for one year. Employers and unions with 100 or more workers will be covered beginning July 2, 1965 and coverage will be extended each year until July 2, 1968 when employers and unions with 25 workers will be covered.)

Not covered by this title are (1) public employers, (2) bona fide private clubs, (3) educational institutions with regard to employees working in educational activities and all employment in religious educational institutions, (4) employers on or near an Indian reservation with regard to preferential treatment of Indians, and (5) religious corporations, institutions, etc., with regard to employees working in connection with religious activities.

When someone believes he has been discriminated against because of race, color, religion, sex, or national origin in any phase of job placement or employment, he may bring his complaint within 90 days to the Equal Employment Opportunity Commission or to the Attorney General.

The Commission will handle his complaint directly, unless the State or locality where the alleged discrimination occurred has fair employment laws. If so, the person complaining must allow the State or local officials no more than 120 days to resolve the matter. If there is no satisfactory conclusion within this time or if the State or locality rejects the complaint before the time is up, the complainant may then go to the Commission, which is authorized to settle valid complaints by conciliation and persuasion. Nothing said during the conciliation proceedings may be made public or used as evidence without the consent of the parties.

If the Commission fails to secure compliance within a period of no more than 60 days, the individual may take his case to a Federal court. This court may appoint an attorney and may exempt the complainant from payment of certain costs. The court, in its discretion, may allow the Attorney General to enter the case.

A worker who thinks he has been discriminated against may take his complaint directly to the Attorney General, who may bring the case before a three-judge court if he believes there is a pattern or practice of resistance to this title.

If the court in either action finds discrimination, it will order the employer, employment agency or union to take corrective action, which may include hiring or reinstating employees with or without back pay.

TITLE VIII: VOTING STATISTICS

The Secretary of Commerce is required to conduct a survey of persons of voting age by race, color, and national origin and to determine the extent to which such persons have registered and voted in such geographic areas as the Commission on Civil Rights recommends.

A similar survey must also be conducted on a nationwide basis in connection with the 1970 Census. No person questioned during such surveys may be compelled to disclose his race, color, religion or national origin and everyone must be advised of his right to refuse to give this information.

TITLE IX: INTERVENTION AND REMOVAL IN CIVIL RIGHTS CASES

The Attorney General is authorized to intervene in any Federal court action seeking relief from the denial of equal protection of the laws on account of race, color, religion or national origin. If a Federal court refuses to accept a civil rights case and sends it back to a State court, this action may be reviewed on appeal.

Title X: Community Relations Service

A Community Relations Service is established in the Department of Commerce to provide assistance to persons or communities requiring help with civil rights problems where discriminatory practices impair constitutional rights or affect interstate commerce. The Service is authorized to cooperate with both public and private agencies, either on its own initiative or upon request from local officials or interested persons in situations where disputes threaten peaceful relations among the citizens of a community.

In addition, the Service is authorized to seek a voluntary settlement of public accommodation complaints which may be referred to it by a Federal Court. The Act directs that all activities of the Service in providing conciliation assistance shall be conducted in confidence and without publicity.

Title XI: Miscellaneous

This title gives a right to jury trial in criminal contempt cases arising out of Titles II, III, IV, V, VI and VII. Title I retains the more limited jury trial provisions of the 1957 Civil Rights Act.

Appropriations are authorized to carry out the Act, and a separability clause provides that the rest of the Act will be unaffected if any portion is invalidated. Another section preserves existing remedies under Federal law. This title also preserves the rights of the States to legislate in the same areas covered by this Act, so long as such legislation is not inconsistent with the purposes of the Act.

12. . . . *And We Shall Overcome*

Lyndon B. Johnson Asks Congress to Extend the Privileges of Citizenship to All—1965

Voting is the foundation stone for all rights. "More than a badge of citizenship and dignity—it is an effective tool for change," Martin Luther King once said.

In 1965 there were still whole counties in which evasion tactics, or intimidation, or both, had successfully disfranchised Negroes. In Selma, Alabama, only 355 Negroes out of 15,000 were registered to vote.

Civil rights leaders organized a protest march from Selma to Montgomery, the state capital, to dramatize demands for voting rights. Outside of Selma, the march was halted—with bloodshed—by mounted possemen and helmeted state troopers.

President Lyndon B. Johnson went before a joint session of Congress on March 15, 1965. In a nationally televised address, he demanded immediate action on legislation he would send to Congress two days later—legislation designed to remove every barrier of discrimination against citizens trying to register and vote. He took the rallying cry of the freedom movement into Congress, "We Shall Overcome," the Negro freedom hymn.

"It is not just Negroes, but it is all of us," the President said, "who must overcome the crippling legacy of bigotry and injustice. *And we shall overcome.*"

His speech was a startling and moving departure from ritual and routine. Other Presidents had sought to advance the cause of civil rights, none had so completely identified himself with the Negro cause, none had made the issue of Negro equality so frankly a moral cause for all Americans and for himself. His daughter, Lynda Bird, summed up the impact of the speech. "It was just like that hymn," she told an interviewer: "'Once to every man and nation comes a moment to decide.'"

The President's written message to Congress reviewed the major steps taken to meet "challenges to the authority of the Constitution"—the Civil Rights Act of 1957, "to challenge through litigation the discriminatory use of vote tests"; the Civil Rights Act of 1960, "to simplify such litigation"; the Civil Rights Act of 1964, "to expedite litigation."

President Johnson declared that "eight years of litigation has made it clear that the prompt and fair registration of qualified Negro citizens cannot be achieved under present litigation in the face of consistent defiance of the laws of Congress."

He asked Congress to enact legislation which would "strike down restrictions to voting in all elections—Federal, State, and local—which have been used to deny Negroes the right to vote"; establish in all states and counties "a simple, uniform standard" of voter registration which will make it impossible to thwart the Fifteenth Amendment; provide adequate power to ensure that Federal officials can perform functions essential to the right to vote whenever State officials deny that right; eliminate the opportunity to delay the right to vote by resort to tedious and unnecessary lawsuits; provide authority to ensure that properly registered voters will not be prohibited from voting.

On March 21, the interrupted march to Montgomery began again—now with 3,000 white and Negro citizens, in what Dr. King called "gigantic witness" to the constitutionally guaranteed right of all citizens to register and vote. By court ruling, in the interest of safety, only 300 were permitted to go the whole trip from the point seven miles out of Selma where U. S. Highway 80 narrowed from four lanes to two. Four days later, on the outskirts of Montgomery, 25,000 Americans from all sections of the country—ministers, rabbis, priests, nuns, students, representatives of organizations, citizens who had never before been "involved"—joined the march for the final three-and-one-half miles. It was a spectacular demonstration of diverse peoples united in common cause.

The longer march goes on, each milestone bringing it closer

to its goal, adding new strength and new assurance of victory.

"Our mission," President Johnson said, "is at once the oldest and the most basic of this country: to right wrong, to do justice, to serve man."

REMARKS OF LYNDON B. JOHNSON
TO A JOINT SESSION OF THE CONGRESS
MARCH 15, 1965

Mr. Speaker, Mr. President, Members of the Congress:

I speak tonight for the dignity of man and the destiny of democracy.

I urge every member of both parties, Americans of all religions and of all colors, from every section of this country, to join me in that cause.

At times history and fate meet at a single time in a single place to shape a turning point in man's unending search for freedom. So it was at Lexington and Concord. So it was a century ago at Appomattox. So it was last week in Selma, Alabama.

There, long-suffering men and women peacefully protested the denial of their rights as Americans. Many were brutally assaulted. One good man, a man of God, was killed.

There is no cause for pride in what has happened in Selma. There is no cause for self-satisfaction in the long denial of equal rights to millions of Americans. But there is cause for hope and for faith in our democracy in what is happening here tonight.

For the cries of pain and the hymns and protests of oppressed people have summoned into convocation all the majesty of this great government of the greatest nation on earth.

Our mission is at once the oldest and the most basic of this country: to right wrong, to do justice, to serve man.

In our time we have come to live with moments of great crisis. Our lives have been marked with debate about great issues; issues of war and peace, of prosperity and depression. But rarely in any time does an issue lay bare the secret heart of America itself. Rarely are we met with a challenge, not to our growth or abundance, our welfare or our security, but rather to the values and the purposes and the meaning of our beloved nation.

The issue of equal rights for American Negroes is such an issue. And should we defeat every enemy, should we double our wealth and conquer the stars, and still be unequal to this issue, then we will have failed as a people and as a nation.

For with a country as with a person, "What is a man profited, if he shall gain the whole world, and lose his own soul?"

There is no Negro problem. There is no Southern problem. There is no Northern problem. There is only an American problem. And we are met here tonight as Americans to solve that problem.

This was the first nation in the history of the world to be founded with a purpose. The great phrases of that purpose still sound in every American heart, North and South: "All men are created equal," "government by consent of the governed," "give me liberty or give me death." Those are not just clever words. Those are not just empty theories. In their name Americans have fought and died for two centuries, and tonight around the world they stand there as guardians of our liberty, risking their lives.

Those words are a promise to every citizen that he shall share in the dignity of man. This dignity cannot be found in a man's possessions, his power or his position. It rests on his right to be treated as a man equal in opportunity to all others. It says that he shall share in freedom, choose his leaders, educate his children, and provide for his family according to his ability and his merits as a human being.

To apply any other test—to deny a man his hopes because of his color or race, his religion or the place of his birth—is not only to do injustice, it is to deny America and to dishonor the dead who gave their lives for American freedom.

Our fathers believed that if this noble view of the rights of man was to flourish, it must be rooted in democracy. The most basic right of all was the right to choose your own leaders. The history of this country, in large measure, is the history of the expansion of that right to all of our people.

Many of the issues of civil rights are very complex and most difficult. But about this there can and should be no argument. Every American citizen must have an equal right to vote. There is no reason which can excuse the denial of that right. There is no duty which weighs more heavily on us than the duty we have to ensure that right.

Yet the harsh fact is that in many places in this country men and women are kept from voting simply because they are Negroes.

Every device of which human ingenuity is capable has been used to deny this right. The Negro citizen may go to register only to be told that the day is wrong, or the hour is late, or the official in charge is absent. And if he persists, and if he manages to present himself to the registrar, he may be disqualified because he did not spell out his middle name or because he abbreviated a word on the application.

And if he manages to fill out an application he is given a test. The registrar is the sole judge of whether he passes this test. He may be asked to recite the entire constitution, or explain the most complex provisions of state laws. And even a college degree cannot be used to prove that he can read and write.

For the fact is that the only way to pass these barriers is to show a white skin.

Experience has clearly shown that the existing process of law cannot overcome systematic and ingenious discrimination. No law that we now have on the books—and I have helped to put three of them there—can ensure the right to vote when local officials are determined to deny it.

In such a case our duty must be clear to all of us. The Constitution says that no person shall be kept from voting because of his race or his color. We have all sworn an oath before God to support and to defend that Constitution. We must now act in obedience to that oath.

Wednesday I will send to Congress a law designed to eliminate illegal barriers to the right to vote.

The broad principle of that bill will be in the hands of the Democratic and Republican leaders tomorrow. After they have reviewed it, it will come here formally as a bill. I am grateful for this opportunity to come here tonight at the invitation of the leadership to reason with my friends, to give them my views, and to visit with my former colleagues.

I have had prepared a more comprehensive analysis of the legislation which I intended to transmit tomorrow but which I will submit to the clerks tonight. But I want to discuss with you now briefly the main proposals of this legislation.

This bill will strike down restrictions to voting in all elections—Federal, State, and local—which have been used to deny Negroes the right to vote.

This bill will establish a simple, uniform standard which cannot be used, however ingenious the effort, to flout our Constitution.

It will provide for citizens to be registered by officials of the United States government if the State officials refuse to register them.

It will eliminate tedious, unnecessary lawsuits which delay the right to vote.

Finally, this legislation will ensure that properly registered individuals are not prohibited from voting.

I will welcome suggestions from all of the members of Congress—and I have no doubt that I will get some—on ways and means to strengthen this law and to make it effective. But experience has plainly shown that this is the only path to carry out the command of the Constitution.

To those who seek to avoid action by their national government in their own communities; who seek to maintain purely local control over elections, the answer is simple:

Open your polling places to all your people.

Allow men and women to register and vote whatever the color of their skin.

Extend the rights of citizenship to every citizen of this land.

There is no constitutional issue here. The command of the Constitution is plain.

There is no moral issue. It is wrong to deny any of our fellow Americans the right to vote.

There is no issue of states rights or national rights. There is only the struggle for human rights.

I have not the slightest doubt what will be your answer.

The last time a President sent a civil rights bill to the Congress it contained a provision to protect voting rights in Federal elections. That civil rights bill was passed after eight long months of debate. And when that bill came to my desk from the Congress, the heart of the voting provision had been eliminated.

This time, on this issue, there must be no delay, no hesitation and no compromise with our purpose.

We cannot, we must not, refuse to protect the right of every American to vote in every election that he may desire to participate in. We ought not, we must not, wait another eight months before we get a bill. We have already waited a hundred years and more, and the time for waiting is gone.

I ask you to join me in working long hours, nights, and weekends if necessary, to pass this bill. And I don't make that request lightly. For from the window where I sit with the problems of our country I am aware that outside this chamber is the outraged conscience of a nation, the grave concern of many nations, and the harsh judgment of history on our acts.

But even if we pass this bill, the battle will not be over. What happened in Selma is part of a far larger movement which reaches into every section and state of America. It is the effort of American Negroes to secure for themselves the full blessings of American life.

Their cause must be our cause too. It is not just Negroes, but it is all of us, who must overcome the crippling legacy of bigotry and injustice.

And we shall overcome.

As a man whose roots go deeply into Southern soil I know how agonizing racial feelings are. I know how difficult it is to reshape the attitudes and the structure of our society.

But a century has passed, more than a hundred years, since the Negro was freed. And he is not fully free tonight.

It was more than a hundred years ago that Abraham Lincoln, a great President of the Republican party, signed the Emancipation Proclamation, but emancipation is a proclamation and not a fact.

A century has passed, more than a hundred years, since equality was promised. And yet the Negro is not equal.

A century has passed since the day of promise. And the promise is still unkept.

The time of justice has now come. I tell you I believe sincerely that no force can hold it back. It is right in the eyes of man and God that it should come. And when it does, I think that day will brighten the lives of every American.

For Negroes are not the only victims. How many white children have gone uneducated, how many white families have lived in stark poverty, how many white lives have been scarred by fear, because we wasted our energy and our substance to maintain the barriers of hatred and terror?

So I say to all of you here, and to all in the nation tonight, that those who appeal to you to hold on to the past do so at the cost of denying you your future.

This great, rich, restless country can offer opportunity and education and hope to all: black and white, North and South, sharecropper and city dweller. These are the enemies: poverty, ignorance, disease. They are the enemies and not our fellow man, not our neighbor. And these enemies too, poverty, disease and ignorance, we shall overcome.

Let none of us look with prideful righteousness on the troubles in another section, or on the problems of our neighbors. There is no part of America where the promise of equality has been fully kept. In Buffalo as well as in Birmingham, in Philadelphia as well as in Selma, Americans are struggling for the fruits of freedom.

This is one nation. What happens in Selma or in Cincinnati is a matter of legitimate concern to every American. But let each of us look within our own hearts and our own communities, and let each of us put our shoulder to the wheel to root out injustice wherever it exists.

As we meet here in this historic chamber tonight, men from the South, some of whom were at Iwo Jima—men from the North who have carried Old Glory to far corners of the world and brought it back without a stain on it—men from the East and West, are all fighting together in Vietnam without regard to religion, or color, or region. Men from every region fought for us across the world twenty years ago. And in these common dangers and these common sacrifices the South made its contribution of honor and gallantry no less than any other region of the great Republic. And I have not the slightest doubt that good men from everywhere in this country, from the Great Lakes to the Gulf of Mexico, from the Golden Gate to the harbors along the Atlantic, will rally together now in this cause to vindicate the freedom of all Americans. For all of us owe his duty; and I believe all of us will respond to it.

Your President makes that request of every American.

The real hero of this struggle is the American Negro. His actions and protests, his courage to risk safety and even to risk his life, have awakened the conscience of this nation. His demonstrations have been designed to call attention to injustice, to provoke change, and to stir reform. He has called upon us to make good the promise of America. And who among us can say that we would have made the same progress were it not for his persistent bravery, and his faith in American democracy.

For at the real heart of battle for equality is a deep-seated belief in the democratic process. Equality depends not on the force of arms or tear gas but upon the force of moral right; not on recourse to violence but on respect for law and order.

There have been many pressures upon your President and there will be others as the days come and go. But I pledge you tonight that we intend to fight this battle where it should be fought: in the courts, and in Congress, and in the hearts of men.

We must preserve the right of free speech and the right of free assembly. But the right of free speech does not carry with it, as has been said, the right to holler fire in a crowded theater. We must preserve the right to free assembly, but free assembly does not carry with it the right to block public thoroughfares to traffic.

We do have a right to protest, and a right to march under conditions that do not infringe the Constitutional rights of our neighbors. And I intend to protect all those rights as long as I am permitted to serve in this office.

We will guard against violence, knowing it strikes from our hands the very weapons with which we seek progress—obedience to law and belief in American values.

In Selma as elsewhere we seek and pray for peace. We seek order. We seek unity. But we will not accept the peace of suppressed rights, or the order imposed by fear, or the unity that stifles protest. For peace cannot be purchased at the cost of liberty.

In Selma tonight, as in every city, we are working for just and peaceful settlement. We must all remember that after this speech I am making tonight, after the police and the FBI and the marshals have all gone, and after you have promptly passed this bill, the people of Selma and the other cities of the nation must still live and work together. And when the attention of the nation has gone elsewhere they must try to heal the wounds and to build a new community. This cannot be easily done on a battleground of violence, as the history of the South itself shows. It is in recognition of this that men of both races have shown such an outstandingly impressive responsibility in recent days.

The bill that I am presenting to you will be known as a civil rights bill. But, in a larger sense, most of the program I am recommending is a civil rights program. Its object is to open the city of hope to all people of all races.

All Americans must have the right to vote. And we are going to give them that right.

All Americans must have the privileges of citizenship regardless of race. And they are going to have those privileges of citizenship regardless of race.

But I would like to remind you that to exercise these privileges takes much more than just legal right. It requires a trained mind and a healthy body. It requires a decent home, and the chance to find a job, and the opportunity to escape from the clutches of poverty.

Of course, people cannot contribute to the nation if they are never taught to read or write, if their bodies are stunted from hunger, if their sickness goes untended, if their life is spent in hopeless poverty just drawing a welfare check.

So we want to open the gates to opportunity. But we are also going to give all our people, black and white, the help they need to walk through those gates.

My first job after college was as a teacher in Cotulla, Texas, in a small Mexican-American school. Few of them could speak English, and I couldn't speak much Spanish. My students were poor and they often came to class without breakfast, hungry. They knew even in their youth the pain of prejudice. They never seemed to know why people disliked them. But they knew it was so, because I saw it in their eyes. I often walked home late in the afternoon, after the classes were finished, wishing there was more that I could do. But all I knew was to teach them the little that I knew, hoping that it might help them against the hardships that lay ahead.

Somehow you never forget what poverty and hatred can do when you see its scars on the hopeful face of a young child.

I never thought then, in 1928, that I would be standing here in 1965. It never occurred to me in my fondest dreams that I might have the chance to help the sons and daughters of those students and to help people like them all over this country.

But now I do have that chance—I'll let you in on a secret—I mean to use it. And I hope that you will use it with me.

This is the richest and most powerful country which ever occupied the globe. The might of past empires is little compared to ours. But I do not want to be the President who built empires, or sought grandeur, or extended dominion. I want to be the President who educated young children to the wonders of their world. I want to be the President who helped to feed the hungry and to prepare them to be taxpayers instead of tax-eaters. I want to be the President who helped the poor to find their own way and who protected the right of every citizen to vote in every election. I want to be the President who helped to end hatred among his fellow men and who promoted love among the people of all races and all regions and all parties. I want to be the President who helped to end war among the brothers of this earth.

And so at the request of your beloved Speaker and Senator from Montana, the Majority Leader, the Senator from Illinois, the Minority Leader, Mr. McCulloch, and other leaders of both parties, I came here tonight—not as President Roosevelt came down one time in person to veto a bonus bill, not as President Truman came down one time to urge the passage of a railroad bill—I came here to ask you to share this task with me and to share it with the people that we both work for. I want this to be the Congress, Republicans and Democrats alike, which did all these things for all these people.

Beyond this great chamber, are the people we serve. Who can tell what deep and unspoken hopes are in their hearts tonight as they sit there and listen. We all can guess, from our own lives, how difficult they often find their own pursuit of happiness, how many problems each little family has. They look most of all to themselves for their futures. But I think that they also look to each of us.

Above the pyramid on the great seal of the United States it says—in Latin—"God has favored our undertaking."

God will not favor everything that we do. It is rather our duty to divine His will. But I cannot help believing that He truly understands and that He really favors the undertaking that we begin here tonight.

"A Triumph for Freedom"

"The time for waiting is gone," President Johnson had said. However, it took almost five months for Congress to pass the Voting Rights Bill he had called for. The House of Representatives passed it on August 3, 1965, by a vote of 328 to 74; the Senate on August 4 by a vote of 79 to 18. It was signed into law two days later.

The act provides for the suspension of literacy tests and for the directed registration of Negro voters by Federal examiners in those states or subdivisions where less than 50 per cent of the voting population was registered or voted in November, 1964. While it does not ban outright the payment of a poll tax, the law declares that such taxes have been used in some areas to abridge the right to vote and directs the Attorney General to initiate suits to test their constitutionality.

The President revived a historic and dramatic custom by going to the Capitol at noon, on August 6, to sign the bill and to order immediate enforcement. His speech, which was broadcast nationally, compressed into a few sentences the history and hope of the occasion:

"Today is a triumph for freedom as huge as any victory won on the battlefield. Today we strike away the last major shackle of those fierce and ancient bonds. Today the Negro story and the American story fuse and blend."